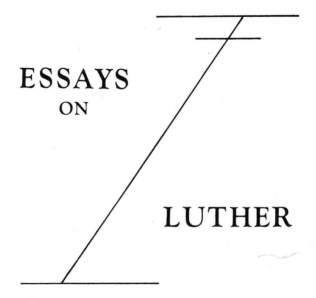

ESSAYS
ON

LUTHER

ESSAYS

ON

LUTHER

Edited by

Kenneth A. Strand

ANN ARBOR PUBLISHERS
1969

ANN ARBOR PUBLISHERS
Campus Village Arcade
611 Church Street
Ann Arbor, Michigan 48104

Ph. 313-665-9130

Preface

In 1962, when Professor Albert Hyma retired from his long and distinguished teaching career of nearly 40 years at the University of Michigan, some 15 of his doctoral graduates and other friends published a Festschrift volume entitled *The Dawn of Modern Civilization: Studies in Renaissance, Reformation and Other Topics Presented to Honor Albert Hyma* (first edition, 1962; second edition, 1964). This volume is now out of print, and it was decided to replace it with some smaller volumes containing various chapters from *Dawn,* plus other materials. The first of these books, *Essays on the Northern Renaissance,* appeared in October, 1968. *Essays on Luther* now appears as a companion volume to that earlier book.

The present publication includes three chapters taken from *Dawn,* one chapter taken from *Andrews University Seminary Studies,* and two new essays. The first four chapters are general historical treatments, and the last two (the new chapters) are historiographical surveys.

In addition to the foregoing, this book incorporates valuable material on Luther from Professor Hyma's Luther biography, which first appeared in a paperback edition under the title *Martin Luther and the Luther Film of 1953* (Ann Arbor, Mich., 1957) and then in hard cover under the title *New Light on Martin Luther* (Grand Rapids, Mich., 1958). Both of these editions are now unfortunately out of print. The material from them which has been included herein appears as an Introduction to the present volume. It has been excerpted and compiled from portions of several chapters in Hyma's Luther biography. We wish to express our gratitude to Professor Hyma for his kind permission to use this material.

It should be pointed out that a small amount of material repeated in connection with the Introduction and various chapters has been allowed to remain, as belonging in each instance to an author's special discussion. This procedure seemed advisable in view of the nature of this publication, in which each chapter stands as a unit by itself as well as contributing to the overall theme.

The editor wishes to express his deep gratitude to each of the contributors to this volume, and also to Ann Arbor Publishers for the kind help and encouragement given.

Kenneth A. Strand

Berrien Springs, Michigan

Contents

Introduction

NEW LIGHT ON LUTHER

By Albert Hyma

(*Editor's Note*: This Introduction includes excerpts from several chapters of Professor Hyma's Luther biography, which appeared in two editions: *Martin Luther and the Luther Film of 1953* [Ann Arbor, Mich., 1957] and *New Light on Martin Luther* [Grand Rapids, Mich., 1958]. Both of these editions are now unfortunately out of print. Materials included here are taken from pp. 13-19, 22, 44, 49-51, 111, 112, 211, 212, 275-277, 279-283 [pagination is the same in both editions], and they are reprinted by permission of Professor Hyma. Regrettably, no brief compilation of this sort can do justice to the wealth of material which appears in Hyma's Luther biography, which is particularly rich in bibliographical allusions and in the presentation of source materials.)

LUTHER'S SO-CALLED "PEASANT MENTALITY"

The widely held view to the effect that Luther always was plagued by a peasant mentality and the poverty of his parents stems from Luther's own words in his Table Talks. The latter were remarks made at the dinner table and reported by a number of students who heard them. In some cases these reports are not reliable, while in others a certain amount of credence can be given to them. Heinrich Fausel in his book, D. Martin Luther Der Reformator im Kampf um Evangelium und Kirche Sein Werden und Wirken: Im Spiegel eigener Zeugnisse (Stuttgart, 1955), presents the remarks about Luther's parents:

My father was in his youth a poor miner. My mother carried all her wood on her back. In that manner did they bring us up. They endured hardship such as the world today would not willingly suffer (Tischreden, 3, 2888a, January 1533).

Duke George of Saxony has in an astonishing manner dragged me down and called me a monster or changeling and the son of a bath maid.... I admit that I am the son of a farmer from Moehra near Eisenach, but nevertheless I have become a Doctor of Biblical Theology and an opponent of the Pope (Tischreden, 3, 3838, April 1538).

I am the son of a farmer. My great-grandfather, my grandfather, and my father were good farmers.... After that my father went to Mansfeld and there he became a mountain miner (Tischreden, 5, 6250, between 1530 and 1539).

It is obvious that this source material is not very helpful, since Luther's father is said to have been a poor miner in his youth, while on another occasion he was declared to have been a farmer, like his own father. Nothing is told here about the residence at Eisleben. The reader gets the impression that Luther's father went directly from Moehra to Mansfeld. It should also be noted that the father soon had so much money at his disposal that he gave to Luther's monastery the equivalent of some $500, while his trip must have cost him a similar amount. He wanted to show his friends how proud he was of Martin's career as a monk, rather than how ashamed he was. And as for his wife's habit of carrying wood on her shoulders, that sort of thing goes on in Germany still. The Germans gleefully pick up sticks in their woods for kindling wood, even after they have become "well heeled." Their frugal habits do not disappear the moment they cease to be poor.

WHY MONASTICISM?

The crucial problem in Luther's youth was how to over-
come the power of evil inclinations and obtain justification before
God. In Magdeburg he had taken a course in religious training
that had led to visions of a saintly life upon earth. At Eisenach
he had met a pious vicar who explained to him the nature of
original sin and the promise of its destruction through monasticism. But he was not certain of which course to follow. Should
he imitate Christ and remain in the world, as He had done, or
should he seek seclusion? His father was not interested in such
questions, and he had persuaded Martin to attend a university,
preferably of course Erfurt, since that was closer to Mansfeld
than was Leipzig. It would be a wonderful thing for the family
if the boy would become a capable attorney. First he must
finish the course in the Liberal Arts, get his A.B. degree and
the A.M. degree. After that would follow the course in the
law school. But Martin was not very enthusiastic. He had visions of emulating the saints of old.

At Erfurt he matriculated under Professor Trutvetter as
"Martinus Ludher ex Mansfelt." That was in the spring of 1501,
and about eighteen months later he finished the course leading
to the A.B. degree. His grades were only average, but in
1505, when he finished the work in the Liberal Arts school, he
ranked second in a class of seventeen. That pleased his ambi-
tious father, who persuaded him to enter the law school as soon
as possible. If he had remained there long he would have lost
his opportunity to become a famous reformer. Not a single
Lutheran church would have been founded.

Erfurt ranked second to Cologne as the largest city in
Germany, and its university came second to that in Cologne.
It was named the German Rome, or miniature Rome. Here the
currents of big business and religion met and mingled. Certainly much could be learned here. The university had about
2,000 students, who lived in dormitories under very strict super-
vision. The religious atmosphere was the dominant factor in
these dormitories, and Luther must have been very much pleased
with his environment. Since he finished both courses in the
minimum amount of time allowed, there need be no question of
his having lived a dissolute life, notwithstanding the insinua-
tions of certain writers of a few decades ago. In recent years
the Roman Catholic authorities have been inclined to treat the

young Luther with reasonable respect. The Protestant biographers have as a rule restrained their enthusiasm for Luther's marked superiority in the realm of ethics and morals. The sources at our disposal are not clear enough to justify either severe condemnation or outright eulogies.

Another controversial subject has been that of humanism versus scholasticism at Erfurt. While a limited amount of humanism was being introduced in Luther's time, the scholastic philosophers retained their ancient authority. It is important to note, however, that the Via Moderna, or the New Way, was more widely accepted at Erfurt than the old school led by Thomas Aquinas. Occam was highly revered, and so were two of his most gifted followers: Pierre d'Ailly and Gabriel Biel. As a direct result Luther became greatly affected by Occamism and nominalism.

It is to be regretted that Luther left very little literature of his own produced in the period from 1501 to 1505, not to mention the earlier years. In this respect he differed greatly from Erasmus. What he is reported to have said many years later in Table Talks is to a great extent unreliable, as we saw, for his remarks were written down by students at the dinner table in his home. In many cases they did not take great pains to be accurate and truthful. Other sources we shall quote below as they illuminate Luther's dramatic decision to enter a monastery and take up the study of theology, instead of law.

Thousands upon thousands of learned pages have been written about the reasons why Luther chose to take the monastic vows. As a rule, his four years as student in the Liberal Arts school are not sufficiently explored, for the promise which Luther made to St. Anna during the thunderstorm near Stotternheim cannot possibly be understood without a study of those four most important years. Martin had gone home to Mansfeld on a vacation during the month of June 1505. On July 2nd, when returning to Erfurt from Mansfeld, at a distance of about five miles from his university, close to the village of Stotternheim, he became frightened by a bolt of lightning. He called upon St. Anna for help, since she was thought to have been particularly useful in such circumstances.

Our most valuable source is his dedication for the work, De Votis Monasticis, addressed to his father in the year 1521. He said: "I was called to this vocation by the terrors of heaven, for neither willingly nor by my own desire did I become a monk; but, surrounded by the terror and agony of a sudden death, I vowed a forced and unavoidable vow." In a letter to Melanchthon written on September 9, 1521, he remarked that he had been "forced rather than drawn into making this vow." Notwithstanding our admission to the effect that the Tischreden, or Table Talks, are not always reliable sources of information, it is generally believed by the experts that the statement made by Luther on July 16, 1539, and published as No. 30 in Otto Scheel's Dokumente, can be trusted. Here we read: "When I had been on my way for fourteen days and was near Stotternheim, not far from Erfurt, I became frightened by a flash of lightning, and exclaimed, 'Help me, dear Saint Anna, I wish to become a monk.' Later I repented of my vow, and many tried to dissuade me from keeping it, but I persevered." In a sermon preached in 1540 Luther said: "When I became a monk, my father was about to go mad. He was greatly displeased, and did not want to give his consent. When I wrote him he answered me, calling me du, whereas before he had called me Ihr, because of my Master's degree."[1]

Perhaps it would not be out of place here to devote a few remarks to the famous biography of Luther by Lucien Febvre, a distinguished professor at the University of Strasbourg: Un destin: Martin Luther (1928), published in English translation as Martin Luther: A Destiny. According to him the best work on Luther was still that by Father Denifle, Luther and Luthertum in der ersten Entwicklung, since the German scholar Ernst Troeltsch had shown how Denifle had been unjustly attacked in spots by a number of well-known authorities. Next Febvre ranked the book by H. Boehmer, Luther im Lichte der neueren Forschung, 4th ed. in 1917. The third place he accorded to the excellent work by Father Grisar, a Jesuit scholar, who was much more moderate in his condemnation of Luther than Denifle had been. It might be noted here that the short volume in English published in 1950 is very important. Febvre ranked Otto Scheel's two volumes of Luther up to 1517 as the fourth. He says in his own biography that much useful work has been done by those who found the early sources defective. It was only natural and proper that scholars should seek to understand Luther's career "from his birth to the entrance into the monastery." Luther's parents were not so poor as had previously been stated, nor was Luther so badly treated as had once been believed. But such matters, said Febvre, were of slight importance. The great mystery was this: What motivated Luther in making that vow? Scheel referred to it as the catastrophe, devoting pp. 241-262 of his first volume to it, and closing that

1. A. Hyma, Luther's Theological Development from Erfurt to Augsburg (New York, 1928), pp. 10-12.

volume with it. Febvre was tremendously intrigued, and he bitterly attacked Denifle for having dared to suppose that Luther
had been immoral. He thought that much more work still remained to be done at this point.[2]

All the experts know that Denifle was much too anxious
to ruin Luther's reputation, but both he and Grisar did an
immense amount of sound research. They understood far better than many Protestant writers that Luther's sudden promise
to enter the monastery was based upon previous experiences
and that he had some good reasons for taking that momentous
step. To say that it was a catastrophe is taking too much for
granted.

Luther often distorted the facts in his early life, as
Schwiebert has frequently indicated. For example, he was unfair to the trivium school at Mansfeld in saying that it was very
disappointing. He also was wrong in telling his father that he
had been forced by an exterior power from heaven to enter the
monastery. There was nothing in the lightning to indicate that
he was being compelled against his will to make the historic
vow. On the contrary, he had been thinking for a long time
about the desirability of entering a monastery. Such was not
unusual for a student in any university at that time. The typical university was dominated by religious practices and views.
It must be rather difficult for our students to visualize life in
the University of Erfurt during the first decade of the sixteenth
century, and for this reason alone numerous books have appeared
recently in which the authors reveal an unfortunate misunder-
standing of early modern education in Europe. A great many
university professors around the year 1500 were monks in excellent standing. Erasmus was for years a traveling monk,
able to move around freely and teach wherever he pleased. He
took advantage of his opportunities and enjoyed them for a long
time. Luther could have done the same. A large proportion
of the best scholars in Europe used to be monks. They led in
historical and scientific research, while their other colleagues
in the great universities shared with them in the dissemination
of useful knowledge. Luther should not have complained to his
father and to Melanchthon about his having been forced to make
that vow. It appears that Luther was consistent in telling Saint
Anna in 1505 that he wished to become a monk.

2. L. Febvre, Un destin: Martin Luther (Paris, 1928), pp. 17-18.
   41-47.

FRIENDSHIP WITH ERASMUS

For a period of about fifteen years Erasmus exerted a wholesome influence upon Luther. The two men had much in common, for their main concern was the reformation of State and Church. They were both of purely Germanic stock and they had both been strongly affected by the Devotio Moderna and by humanism. About Gerard Zerbolt, the greatest thinker in the Devotio Moderna, Luther said that he had given the best description of man's fall from divine grace. As for Gabriel Biel, Rector of the Brethren of the Common Life at Butzbach, Luther said that he had learned his famous book, Canon of the Mass, almost entirely by heart. When Erasmus and Luther finally become hostile to monasticism they agreed that the Brethren of the Common Life had set them a better example than the monks. Luther was even more favorable to the pious brotherhood than was Erasmus. In 1532 he wrote as follows about the men at Herford:

"I dare not indulge in great wishes, but if all other things were in as good a condition as the brethren-houses, the Church would be much too blessed even in this life. Your dress and other commendable usages do not injure the Gospel, but are rather of advantage to it, assailed as in these days it is by reckless and unbridled spirits who know only how to destroy, but not to build up."

And in the same year the German reformer addressed the magistrates of Herford in the following manner: "Inasmuch as the Brethren and Sisters were the first to begin the Gospel among you, lead a creditable life, have a decent and well-behaved congregation, and at the same time faithfully teach and hold the pure word, may I affectionately entreat your worships not to permit any dispeace or molestation to befall them, on account of their still wearing the religious dress, and observing old and laudable usages not contrary to the Gospel? For such monasteries and brethren-houses please me beyond measure. Would to God that all monastic institutions were like them! Clergymen, cities, and countries would then be better served, and more prosperous than they now are."[1]

---

1. C. Ullmann, <u>Reformers Before the Reformation</u>, Vol. II, pp. 176-177. The originals are found in Luther's Letters, edited by E. L. Enders, Vol. II, pp. 146-147; Erlangen ed., no. 386, Weimer ed., no. 1900.

It would be a fascinating task to search into the origins of Erasmus' opinions and to trace the influence exerted by him in various countries. At the present time, however, very little can be said with certainty. Even the year of his birth is not positively known, although the available evidence points to 1469 as the probable date. From 1475 to 1486 he was strongly affected by the Brethren of the Common Life in Deventer and elsewhere. This semi-monastic organization had produced several important mystical writings and also some new methods in education. But it so happened that Erasmus grew intensely interested in humanism pure and simple. In 1486 or 1487 he entered a monastery, named Steyn, located near Gouda, in the vicinity of the place where Gerard, his father, and Margaret, his mother, had once lived. Monasticism attracted him, because it would enable him to study. His later references to this experience are in fact very misleading. It is also wrong to assume, as most of his biographers have done, that he disliked the monastic life. His first booklet, entitled On the Contempt of the World, and his Book Against the Barbarians in their original form are eulogies on both monasticism and humanism.

Erasmus left Steyn in 1492 or 1493, but he remained an Augustinian Canon Regular until the monastic vows became so obnoxious to him that he obtained a dispensation from Pope Leo X, absolving him from the same (1517).

After the year 1506 he joined the majority of the humanists in ridiculing the monks. In many other ways he resembled the typical humanists: He showed practically no interest in the well-being of the common people, and he consistently sought the friendship of wealthy patrons. He frequently resorted to flattery. Nor did he scruple at deliberate lying in order to advance himself. Science meant almost nothing to him. Dogma, on the other hand, meant little more. He was always greatly interested in religion, but rarely in doctrine.

His writings plainly show how his mind developed from year to year. Since they were numerous enough to fill a dozen folio volumes, only a few can be mentioned here. In 1501 he composed the Handbook of the Christian Knight, which reflects the wholesome influence of Colet. Practical religion is here contrasted with empty formalism.

The next important work was the Familiar Colloquies, a textbook of Latin style, based very largely on Erasmus' own experiences. The stories are in the form of conversations and aim to impart much useful information about religious, social, and political conditions. The first edition was composed in 1497, but it was not published until 1518. It was enlarged from time to time. The same was done with the Adagia, or Adages, a collection of proverbs culled from the classics, published for the first time in 1500, and containing 818 adages, while the edition of 1508 counted 3260 proverbs.

The most widely read work of Erasmus was his celebrated Moriae Encomium, or The Praise of Folly, completed in 1509 and published in 1511. This little book made Erasmus the most famous scholar in the world and entitled him to bear the name of prince of the humanists. Here he satirized the principal follies of mankind, but, unlike the authors of The Letters of Obscure Men he did not single out any individual for special mention.

Those who now read the book may feel somewhat disappointed, for it lacks the positive element of a reformer's constructive plans. It was easy for Erasmus to criticize existing conditions, but he disliked the work of constructing different conditions. Luther was moved to write in 1532: "When Erasmus wrote his Folly, he begot a daughter like himself, for he turns, twists, and bites like an awl; but he, as a fool, has written true folly."

One should bear in mind, however, that Erasmus could be serious when he chose. He contributed much to scholarship and to educational reform. He knew the value of ridicule and through his Praise of Folly he was able to reach thousands of well-educated men and women who became convinced of the need of thorough-going changes in church and state. He did not wear a martyr's crown, nor did he lead an army into battle. But he proved that in many cases the pen is mightier than the sword. Moreover, there have always been numerous eminent thinkers who have maintained that the reforms proposed by Erasmus, although not carried out by him, were intended for an age of greater enlightenment than that which witnessed his struggle with ignorance and superstition, with bigotry and intolerance. It is true, at least, that Erasmus for a period of about twenty years was the prince of the humanists and the intellectual king of Europe.

Erasmus embodied elements of both Transalpine humanism and Protestantism. Like Wessel Gansfort, whom he and Luther so greatly admired, he fully comprehended the existing abuses in the Church. When contemporaries said that he had "laid the egg of ecclesiastical reform" and that "Luther hatched it," they expressed a profound truth, though the chicken behaved badly later on, according to Erasmus. The sale of indulgences, simony, nepotism, empty formalism, the indolence and immorality of many monks and parish priests, the indifference of several popes and of numerous bishops to true religion,—all of this he thoroughly exposed in his writings. He prepared the field in which the great reformers of both camps—Protestants and Roman Catholics—labored to reform the Church. But where he and other learned humanists differed from Luther and Calvin and Loyola was in their attitude toward the importance of dogma and ecclesiastical institutions.

Erasmus spoke in the year 1515 as hundreds of well-known churchmen have spoken in the twentieth century. In his opinion it mattered little whether the miracles recorded in the Bible had actually happened or not. As for the doctrines of transubstantiation, of purgatory, and of justification by faith and works, he believed that they might be interpreted in various ways. He thought it was very foolish for anybody to stake his career on the definition of doctrines, and he said on many occasions that to imitate the life of Jesus was far more important than to argue about dogma. Those who considered him a coward lost sight of his great intellectual capacity.

Nearly all the negative points of Protestantism were very widely advertised by Erasmus before Luther discussed them in writing. Luther never published his lectures on the Epistle of Paul to the Romans. Those on the Psalms were also little known before 1517, whereas the Colloquies and The Praise of Folly by Erasmus were the talk of the day in thousands of places.

ADDITIONAL NOTE ON ERASMUS BY PROFESSOR HYMA
(December, 1968)

Preserved Smith on page 258 of his admirable biography of Erasmus published in 1923 by Harper presents the following report concerning the phenomenal success attained by Erasmus' most famous books:

> During the author's lifetime the *Folly* was printed in nine different cities, and in each of two of them, Venice and Cologne, by three separate publishers. The New Testament was printed by seven publishers at Basel alone.

And on page 125 Smith says this:

> The *Praise of Folly* won an immediate and striking success. Its publication marked the real beginning of that immense international reputation that put its author on a pinnacle in the world of letters hardly surpassed or even approached by anyone later save Voltaire.

We may safely add that Voltaire was vastly overshadowed by Erasmus after all. The latter was quoted and consulted by the highest potentates in the fields of politics and religion both.

LUTHER'S BIBLE TRANSLATION

One of Luther's most important labors was translation of the Bible into virile German. Although fourteen editions had already appeared in High German and four others in Low German, Luther was the first to produce a translation that met the demands of the masses. He literally produced the modern language of Germany. Being situated in the center of the German-speaking countries, about half-way between North and South, and also between East and West, he was destined to become a tremendous figure in the field of philology. At the Wartburg he translated the whole of the New Testament, using some of the earlier translations and improving upon them all as he went along.

It is remarkable that Luther's most important contribution to the making of German civilization in modern times has been treated with indifference on the part of many theologians and even historians. His creation of modern High German is a tremendous feat, worthy of untold eulogy. But endless thousands of pages have been written about his little disputes with insignificant persons, as if those were the main theme of Luther's life at the Wartburg. Even his debate with Eck at Leipzig is not a matter of world-shaking importance, as compared with his translation of the New Testament. What he had in mind particularly was the proper diction, the choice of certain phrases. He was thinking about his own relatives near the castle. They were the sort of people who were dwelling in darkness to a certain extent, because so much of the ritual of the Church was in Latin and the translations of the New Testament in their language were unsatisfactory. His linguistic work is of staggering significance, and this matter is usually best explained in those departments in which the German languages are taught. Among our best theologians the situation is seldom understood.

Germany really had two different languages, the Low German and the High German. Until recent times the Low German was used by millions of German citizens. It was a literary language, not a mere dialect. The historian must use the city chronicles of Cologne, Hamburg, Berlin, Bremen, Luebeck, Magdeburg, Duisburg, Duesseldorf, Muenster, Aachen, Rostock, and Danzig to view this matter in its proper aspect. In all of these important cities the language used was Low German, which was very similar to Dutch and Flemish. It was Luther who destroyed Low German as a real language.

Luther completed his New Testament at the Wartburg Castle in 1522. He took the manuscript with him to Wittenberg in the spring of 1522, and after having checked everything with Melanchthon, he published it in September, 1522. Assisted by Melanchthon and others, he translated the Old Testament in the period between 1522 and 1534. In the latter year he published his first complete translation of the Bible. Not satisfied with this work, he consulted some of his colleagues in the University of Wittenberg and prepared two more complete translations of the Bible. The second of the two was not published until after his death. In 1523 he had published the first five books of the Old Testament and the rest appeared a few years later. First came what he called The Second Part of the Old Testament. It did not give the date nor the authorship on the title page. But we are reasonably sure that the date was 1523. It contained all the books from Joshua to Esther. In September or October of 1524 he published what he called The Third Part of the Old Testament. Like the other two volumes it was in folio form and profusely illustrated. In 1526 he published one of the prophets, and in 1528 two more. In 1529 the Wisdom of Solomon was published, followed in 1530 by the Book of Daniel. In February, 1532, he published another volume entitled The Prophets all in German. Luther spent a great deal of time on the Book of Psalms, which he published in 1529. The edition of his own of 1524 he considered very unsatisfactory, which it was up to a certain point. He kept on revising the Psalms for several years more.

The second edition of the complete Bible appeared in 1541. The edition of 1545, which has often been considered the final work of Luther, was merely a reprint, while the actual third revision was printed in 1546, shortly after Luther's death. For more than three hundred years, almost until the end of the nineteenth century, practically all of the Lutheran scholars accepted the 1545 edition as the official text for the Lutheran churches. But in recent years it has been shown that the 1546 edition should have been so regarded.

Luther always looked upon the Bible as a unit, and he tried to explain all the contents of the Old Testament as leading up to the Gospel in the New Testament. The crucifixion of Christ, according to him, was the central theme of the whole Bible. In the second place, Luther felt that the translator must be very careful with the choice of his words. He must consult all the grammatical rules of the Hebrew in the Old Testament and of the Greek in the New Testament. At the same time he must be aware of the great difficulties involved in trying to find the proper terminology. In many cases, as all

linguists know, certain words cannot be translated literally.
Luther did not perfect a literal translation of the Bible, but he
created, as we saw above, a new language for the German people.

Because of his fame as a scholar and his tremendous
linguistic talent, the sale of his translations were enormous.
That of his New Testament published in 1522 went through numerous editions, so that by 1534, when the complete Bible was
first published, about 200,000 copies had been sold. In Wittenberg alone not fewer than 19 High-German and 4 Low-German
editions were printed of the whole Bible. These were reprinted
83 times in High German and 19 times in Low German in Wittenberg alone during Luther's lifetime. From 1522 to Luther's
death in 1546 about 430 complete or partial Bibles were published in Germany. It had been estimated that each edition
was made up of about 2000 copies. About 500 woodcuts were
prepared for the Luther Bible. During Luther's lifetime alone
about 104 illustrated Bibles were published. Some of the most
famous artists collaborated in the production of these remarkable Bibles by Luther.[1]

---

1. See E. G. Schwiebert, Luther and His Times, p. 662.

A NEW APPRAISAL

Many faults in Luther's character have recently been exposed by Protestant historians and theologians. In the meantime the Catholic scholars have not ceased to defend themselves against unfair criticism on the part of Protestant writers. It has become very difficult to derive at a proper evaluation of Luther's career and works. The latest theory has been to the effect that when Luther was a comparatively old man he made statements that do not compare favorably with those of earlier years.

It would seem that Luther was no worse at the age of sixty than twenty years earlier. As a matter of fact, his behavior in the period from 1518 to 1526 was such that he lost numerous intelligent friends in those fateful years. The loss of the Rhine Valley and all European lands to the west of that river and south of the Alps was partly the result of his actions and thoughts before the year 1527. What he wrote about Erasmus and Zwingli, what he said against the peasants in 1525, the manner in which he condemned King Henry VIII of England in 1522 and the Pope before that, and his discussion of monastic vows in the year 1521—these and many other matters harmed his cause tremendously. In 1535 his most devoted friend of the past, Philip Melanchthon, gave up his belief in Luther's doctrine of the enslaved will and total depravity. He shuddered many times whenever the great master thundered forth with his violent language. But what nearly all biographers have consistently overlooked is Luther's remarkable doctrines and theories in his last three years.

After we have studied the Augsburg Confession, the Schwabach Articles, the Marburg Articles, the Wittenberg Concord, the Worms Articles, the Regensburg Book, the Swiss and French creeds, besides a host of others, it seems refreshing to read Luther's own simple creed of the year 1545. In that intriguing document he could freely express his innermost convictions. He said that there were three sacraments, including Penance. He reaffirmed his opinion on the powers of secular rulers, denying once more that they had the right to determine what their subjects should believe in the field of religion. His original view on the eucharist he now stated so plainly that nobody would henceforth be confused about it. Christ's natural body was actually present in a physical manner during the communion service. The theologians at the University of Louvain had become "damned heathen." True, but this was merely a repetition of similar statements issued long ago. The Zwinglians were also damned, and the Anabaptists might be killed with impunity, although he had stated on several occasions that no-body should be punished with the death penalty for merely re-ligious opinions.   He still said very mean things about the papacy, and that again was a repetition of what he had uttered in 1520.

What annoys Protestant writers the most at the present time is Luther's admission of his failure to improve the moral standards of both princes and subjects, high and low, rich and poor.   Leon Francis in his booklet, The Martin Luther Motion Picture, devotes the last two pages to quotations from Luther's own pen, written down near the end of his life, when he realized how hard it was for him to correct the evil ways of mankind. He said among other things: "We can then expect that after having driven away the monks, we shall see arise a race seven times worse than the former."   That was a very naughty thing to say, and the following was little better: "We deserve that our Evangelicals should now be seven times worse than they were before.   Because, after having learned the Gospel, we steal, tell lies, deceive, eat and drink to excess, and practice all manner of vices."   Amazing to many readers must be this frank admission: "Men are now more avaricious, unmerciful, impure, insolent ...than formerly under the Pope."

These quotations from Luther do not prove anything ex-cept that he had the habit of exaggerating the truth.   That was a very old habit on his part, and he shared it with such dis-tinguished men as Erasmus and Ulrich von Hutten.   When in 1521 he advised Melanchthon to "sin powerfully," he had no idea that this statement would be quoted a thousand times against him.

But to ignore Luther's remarks is also stupid.   The whole truth must be revealed.   When he no longer was interested in pleasing men in high places, he could freely express his senti-ments and convictions, and such he did copiously.   He was a child of his environment, ready to utter horrible condemnations of what others had said and done, "quick at the trigger" in the battle for his cause.   Before the year 1510 he did not know how bad was the life of the average king or duke or count.   Only after having become famous he saw what was going on, notwith-standing his urgent pleas for moral rearmament.   In his naive way he thought that he could win the king of England for his denomination, and he also felt that now all the bad boys in high places must listen carefully to his advice.   When he discovered that even his most devoted friends among the princes would not give up their bad habits he was profoundly shocked.   Not being a good diplomat and having of course no thought about the ver-dict of posterity, he rushed into print with unseemly statements and false accusations.   How did he know what God thought of the Anabaptists?   And who was he to judge the fate of a man like Oecolampadius?

On May 5, 1542, he wrote to Philip of Hesse that his two powerful friends, Counts Gerhard and Albrecht of Mansfeld were still fighting each other. Would Philip please see what he could do to stop this? Luther devoted the last days of his life to the same task, whereas Grisar reasoned that Luther left the campus at Wittenberg partly because he felt that he was not properly appreciated there.[1]

On April 13, 1542, Luther addressed a very pessimistic letter to his old friend Amsdorf, in which he complained about the brawls occasioned by Duke Maurice of Saxony.[2] Amsdorf must not think that this is his fault. Germany's disasters are caused by secular rulers, particularly this Maurice, "the foolhardy, furious youth." And in Wuerttemberg it is not Schwenckfeld that must be held responsible for the disorders but rather a man named Mohr. However, there are also other troubles, such as those resulting from the teachings of Muenzer, Carlstadt, Zwingli, and Seckendorff.[3]

On July 25, 1542, Luther admitted that unspeakable crimes had been committed "in Our Church." This was obviously the work of Satan. On October 9, 1542, he told Jacob Propst in Bremen that Germany was full of scoundrels and tyrants.[4] On August 31, 1543, he wrote to Christopher Froschauer at Zurich: "As for the arduous labors of your preachers, with whom I cannot have friendship, they are all in vain, since they are all going to perdition. . . . They will share the same fate as Zwingli." What worried him especially in the year 1543 was the alliance between the Turks and the French. According to Bainton's biography, Luther had changed this, and henceforth (that is, after about 1525) the French no longer dared to ally with the Turks. On the contrary, the situation was worse than before. And as for the Pope, he must have refused to listen to Luther, who testified himself to the fact that in February 1544 not only the pontiff but also France and the Venetians conspired against the Emperor. In April 1544 the French had 30,000 Turkish troops under their command, collected in Africa and not in Asia, with which they were about to invade Luxembourg, or else Trier.[5]

Another remarkable episode was the imprisonment of Henry of Brunswick by John Frederick of Saxony and Philip of

1. H. Grisar, Martin Luther (1950), p. 568.
2. A. Hyma, article on Maurice of Saxony in the New Schaff-Herzog Encyclopedia of Religious Knowledge, 1955 ed.
3. Briefwechsel, Weimar ed., Vol. X (1947), pp. 48–49, 61.
4. Weimar ed., Vol. X, 156: "Exemplum tamen est a Deo propositum non solum tyrannis nostri seculi (sicuti omnium seculorum exempla sunt tyrannorum), sed etiam contemptoribus verbi, quorum plena est Germania."
5. Ibid., Vol. X, p. 553.

Hesse.   Numerous persons had requested that Luther write these princes and persuade them to release their prisoner.   So he finally released for publication his last printed work (1545), in which he said some interesting things about the political situation in Germany.   He did not recommend that Henry of Brunswick be set free, for the latter had been condemned by God for his attempt to help the forces of the Counter-Reformation.   "We are not, thanks to God, made out of stone, nor iron.   No Christian must wish another man the infliction of God's anger, not even the Turks, nor the Jews, nor his enemies.   No demon may wish such a thing to be done to another demon.   It is too much, eternal anger.   Against that everybody must pray for everybody, and it is compulsory to do so.   I would gladly have seen the Cardinal of Mainz saved, but he would not listen and has gone to damnation.   May God protect all human beings against such a demise.   Similarly, we must love our enemies and forgive them and be merciful, so that the love and mercy shall not be false.   I wish that the prisoner from Brunswick were the king of France and his son the king of England, for what harm would that do to me?   But to recommend that he be set free, I cannot do.   He has lost the trust of others.   Since God has inflicted punishment upon him, who would dare to release him?   This could be done only after he had repented of his evil deeds and had shown improvement, lest we should tempt God. "

Luther compares the recent event with the relation between Ahab and King Benhadad of Syria.   The King of Israel set the latter free, which was all wrong.   Benhadad was God's enemy, and so is Henry of Brunswick, for he had behind him "the Pope and the whole body of the papal power. "   At the Diet of Worms in 1521 these people issued their edict against the Gospel, which they refused to suspend at the Diet of Speyer, though the Emperor would gladly have done so.   Again, at the Diet of Augsburg in 1530 they combined against us.   Since they failed to get the Emperor to execute their desires they wrote to each other that they must seemingly support him and threaten him with dire results if he did not carry out their demands. They formed what they call a defensive league, as if powerful forces were bent upon an attack.   But neither Emperor nor Pope showed any desire to hurt a hair on their bodies.   We on our side begged without ceasing for the maintenance of peace , which we were never able to obtain.   They were the people who started an offensive alliance against us.   We, not they, were condemned through excommunication and edict.   A defensive league is forbidden by imperial laws.   But they are the dear children who cannot commit sin, even when they trample upon God and the Emperor.   We are sinners when we offer our bodies

and lives in the service of God and the Emperor. We are not
merely dealing with Henry of Brunswick but with the whole
Behemoth and forces of the papacy. We know that the Pope
and his satellites cannot be converted, and so all they can do
is to comfort each other.

As for the clergy among the Roman Catholics, they had
better do penance and ask for guides to show them how to do
this. The sins committed by them are numerous, as has been
shown at the Diet of Regensburg. Particularly bad was the in-
vasion of Protestant areas around Goslar, where murder and
destruction were rampant. The list of misdemeanors is very
large and hellfire has been earned by many. In short, the
papists want all the Protestants killed, in body and soul. On
the other hand, we want them all to be saved together with us.
"Which side will be justified before God can easily be determined. "

God has given us a great triumph over our enemies, but
we may not assume that we have earned this triumph. No, we
have not done so very well. Among us there are many who
despise the Word of God and show great ingratitude for their
blessings. The thirst for capital gain is so strong now that
even among the most humble beings a person with only 100
gulden wants to invest this and expects to make 15 or 20 in no
time at all. Common laborers have become so vain and so
worldly that they all engage in usury, take advantage of their
neighbors, steal, cheat, and lie. "It is a wonder that the earth
still carries us. Yes, I say it, we have not earned these blessings, nor our recent political triumph, nor God's protection
against the devil and his cohorts. " But we have one advantage,
that is, God's pure Word, unadulterated; also the Holy Spirit.
There must be among us a few genuine Christians who have
real faith. Such faith cannot be without good works. For
Christ says in John XV: "He who dwells in Me and I in him,
shall bring forth many fruits. " And He says in John XIV: "If
you dwell in Me and My word in you, pray for what you wish
and it shall be given unto you. " And in Mark XI: "All things
are possible to those who believe. "

Such an advantage the papists do not have, for among them
there is not only a contempt of God's Word but also persecu-
tion of those who accept that Word. Their idolatry is well
known, and so are their evil deeds. Their creed is against
God, impure and full of diabolical lies. For that reason they
cannot possibly acquire real faith. Where the faith is not right
there can be no good works, and everything that people try is
damned and altogether in vain, including suffering, fasting, prayers, alms, and all other forms of asceticism and garments
worn. For this reason we need not worry about their prayers,

just as Elijah did not have to worry about the prayers offered
by his enemies to Baal. The same is true of all the labors in
the monasteries and convents. The monks and nuns do not
know how to pray and do not want to pray as long as they do
not have the saving faith.

At the end of his treatise Luther refers once more to
political developments. Maurice of Saxony, the son-in-law of
Philip of Hesse, is now entitled to the territories which Henry
of Brunswick wanted to seize, notably the former archbishopric
of Magdeburg and the former bishopric of Halberstadt. The last
sentence is the famous statement by Jesus in John XIV: "He
that believes in Me shall do the works that I do."[6]

This curious mixture of politics and religion is a good
summary of Luther's career. He continually quoted the Scriptures and used the sacred text to show how certain Lutheran
princes were entitled to their recently acquired possessions.
In his opinion millions of fellow-Protestants were plainly head-
ing for eternal damnation, while nearly all Roman Catholics
were in serious danger of the same fate. His final publication
was not very different from those that had appeared some twenty
years earlier. It showed that he knew "how to play ball" with
the secular rulers whose aid he needed. The reader may well
wonder how Luther wished to apply the inspiring words of Jesus
to the effect that "greater works than these shall you do."
Those were obviously spiritual works, not political victories.
Not a single Protestant knew how to do this in Luther's time.

Professor W. J. Kooiman has recently written a Dutch
biography of Luther. After having appeared in a German translation, it was published in New York by the Philosophical Library under the title of By Faith Alone: the Life of Martin
Luther (1955). Kooiman presents a scholarly appraisal of Luther's last years, saying that during those years Luther "was
particularly harsh and uncompromising." He refers particularly
to the book entitled Against the Papacy of Rome, Which Was
Founded by the Devil. His conclusion on p. 201 is as follows:
"There is no doubt that this gross violence was connected with
his physical health, for he was worn out and could no longer
stand up to the difficulties which came pouring in from all
sides."

But it should not be overlooked that long before 1535
did Luther call the Pope the Anti-Christ, as we know. Moreover, Luther wrote some very fine treatises after 1535. In
1521 he was violent in denouncing King Henry VIII of England,
and in 1545 he was sometimes charitable when composing certain letters and short treatises.

---

6. Weimar ed., Vol. LIV (1928), pp. 389-411.

HISTORY

Chapter 1

LUTHER AND THE PEASANTS' WAR: A BRIEF SUMMARY[1]

By ROBERT N. CROSSLEY

(Reprinted from *Dawn of Modern Civilization*, pp. 129-142)

O NE of the most disturbing events which occurred during the first decade of the Protestant Reformation in Germany was the Great Peasants' War of 1524-1526.[2] This war, revolt, or rebellion had a profound influence on Luther the man as well as Luther the leader of the new Evangelical Movement. The student of the Reformation cannot help but be impressed by the storm of criticism which Luther's actions during the war aroused as well as the great wave of apologetic and defensive tracts and articles put out by his supporters ever since that time. In my opinion, however, the Peasants' War cannot be disassociated from two earlier uprisings in the life of Luther: The Wittenberg Disturbances of 1521-1522 and the Knights' Revolt of 1522-1523. In order to challenge his severe critics and also to meet the arguments of his supersensitive defenders, these three uprisings have to be taken together in assessing Luther's position and actions during this formative period in his career of Reformer.[3] However, inasmuch as such an examination would be impossible in this short paper, I will concentrate on the Peasants' War, making only brief references to the early fracases of 1521-1523.

The years 1521-1526 were five of the most important years in the life of Luther. He had appeared before the Diet of Worms and as a result of that appearance had been forced to go into hiding at the Wartburg. However, he was not to stay at the Wartburg long. After approximately one year he returned once more to Wittenberg to resume his position on the faculty of the

University and his leadership of the new reform movement. He had returned principally because of disturbing reports he had received concerning the radical nature of the reform movement under Karlstadt, Zwilling and the Zwickau prophets.[4] Apparently they had pushed aside Philip Melanchthon and had become the leaders in Luther's absence. Once this uprising was quelled (no other time was Luther more brilliant or more forceful), Luther could resume his personal leadership. That same year Luther was also faced with the Knights' Revolt, and again he demonstrated that even in the political sphere he would not be forced into taking action against the legally constituted authorities—not even by those who considered themselves staunch supporters of the Saxon reformer.

Meanwhile, in parts of southern Germany, peasant unrest was beginning to show itself. This unrest was to become manifest in the great revolt of 1524-1526, a revolt which was to influence Luther tremendously. In August, 1524, the peasants on the lands of the Count of Lupfen near the Black Forest had been ordered by the countess to pick berries. Under terms of the contract between lord and peasant, these tillers of the soil were to be exempt from such labor on church holidays and also during the harvest season. A deputation of peasants presented themselves to the count and petitioned that the order concerning the berries be withdrawn. The deputation further stated that they would refuse to abide by the order. This rather innocuous event was the spark that set aflame most of southern and central Germany and even parts of northern Germany. Bands of peasants were formed, and petitions were presented to their lords; if the demands were rejected, violence occurred. Manor houses, farm buildings, monasteries, and even churches, were looted; and although the bloodshed was not great, the disturbance was becoming exceedingly widespread. In the spring of 1525 a so-called peasant parliament met at Memmingen to consider a general petition or list of demands to be presented to the princes of Germany. From this peasant parliament there emerged the famous Twelve Articles of the Peasants of Swabia.[5] However, not all peasant groups subscribed to this list, nor was there any real unity among the peasants. The word "war" is really a misnomer; there were a series of outbreaks, and numerous lists of demands were presented to the local lords. However, as a result of the meeting at Memmingen, the peasant leaders there assembled did prepare to send copies of the Twelve Articles to leading men in Germany for comment and hoped-for approval. One of the men who received a copy was Martin Luther. From the time that Luther received his copy of these Twelve Articles, chronology plays an important role in a study of the Reformer's position with regard to the revolt.

After considerable deliberation Luther sat down and wrote a reply to the Twelve Articles—his *An Exhortation to Peace Based on the Twelve Articles of the Peasants of Swabia.*[6] This tract by Luther is of the utmost importance because of its moderation and good sense. The tract is divided into two main parts: (1) An address to the princes of Germany, and (2) an address to the peasants. In the first part Luther "pulls no punches" concerning the stupidity, ignorance, and evil-doing of some of the princes. In fact, he says quite clearly that the princes are responsible for the outbreak of the revolt. If they had treated their peasants more humanely—in a more Christian manner— the peasants never would have risen against their lawful masters. Part One is quite forthright; it constitutes a rather bitter attack against those members of the nobility who were more interested in their own material possessions and comfort than in the welfare of the peasants entrusted to their care.

However, it is from Part Two that some criticism of Luther arises. In this section directed to the peasants, he admonishes them to shun violence and to resort to peaceful means for accomplishing the reforms which they ask. He then turns to the Articles themselves. After saying in effect that the princes were really wrong and were the true cause of the revolt, he refuses to discuss all of the articles. Rather, he treats only those few concerning the right of the community to appoint and support its own pastor and the article on the abolition of serfdom. Luther recognizes the right of the congregation to elect its own pastor; but the congregation and the community could not legitimately set aside tithes for the pastor's support since these tithes belonged legally to the government. To do so would be an act of robbery, which should be punished by the authorities. If the congregation persisted in choosing its own pastor, it did have the option or right of moving away and establishing the congregation elsewhere.

In replying to the article concerning the abolition of serfdom, Luther considered this demand to be wrong. Freedom was not a carnal thing; he believed that temporal freedom could not flourish unless there were some free, some serfs, some enslaved. As far as the other articles were concerned (the free use of woods, streams, meadows, and the village commons; and the right of pregnant women to have fish from the ponds), Luther said that these articles were for the lawyers—he himself was only a theologian, not trained in these matters and hence was not competent to judge them.

The chief criticism levied against Luther concerning this first tract of the Peasants' War was his vacillating position. Yet when one seriously examines this tract in the context of time and events, it was not vacillating. On the contrary, it was a moderate document, designed to prevent the outbreak of violence; and it called upon all parties in the dispute to use good judgment and moderation in their future actions.

This tract was published in April, 1525, and had wide circulation throughout the Germanies. In late April and again in early May Luther had the opportunity to travel throughout some of the areas which were witness to the Peasant Revolt. These two trips were indeed first-class educational experiences for the former Augustinian monk, as he saw some of the devastation accomplished by roving bands of peasants and as he also had opportunity to talk with resident eye-witnesses to the destruction. He was informed that there seemed to be a madness among these peasants; that they were far more interested in looting and pillaging the wine cellars than in getting their demands accepted by the local nobility.

Also, while he was in the city of Borna, Luther experienced hecklers in an audience. During a sermon intended to quiet the storm in this area, he was, in fact, almost drowned out by such hecklers. This experience was shocking to him, and one can almost date his antagonism from this moment. After the incident in Borna, Luther's letters (particularly to John Ruehl, the court councillor to the Count of Mansfeld and a close friend of Luther) include rather strong denunciations of the peasant movement and particularly of the radical leaders of these simple tillers of the soil.[7] It is likely that in the audience that day were followers of men like Muenzer or some other radical leader who had been preaching social, economic, and political reform which resulted in inflaming the peasant groups to violence. In any case, when Luther returned to Wittenberg, he immediately began the composition of his *Against the Murdering and Thieving Hordes of Peasants.* By May 31, 1525, the tract was completed, and, it is believed, already in the hands of the publisher. In examining this tract, one can see the anger dripping from the Reformer's pen. He determined that this new evil—the revolt—should be stamped out. Here is what he had to say:[8]

> Therefore, dear lords, here is a place where you can release, rescue, help. Have mercy on these poor people! Stab, smite, slay, whoever can. If you die in doing it, well for you! A more blessed death can never be yours, for you die in obeying the divine Word and commandment in Romans xiii, and in loving service of your neighbor, whom you are rescuing from the bonds of hell and of the devil. And so I beg everyone who can to flee from the peasants as from the devil himself; those who do not flee, I pray that God will enlighten and convert. As for those who are not converted, God grant that they may have neither fortune nor success. To this let every pious Christian say, Amen! For this prayer is right and good, and pleases God; this I know. If anyone thinks this too hard, let him remember that rebellion is intolerable and

that the destruction of the world is to be expected every
hour.

This writing caused a great storm in Germany, particularly
among the peasant bands and among the peasant leaders such as
Karlstadt. It has been criticized for its violent language and uncompromising position as well as for the timing of its publication.
Luther began preparing this tract in early May, 1525, upon
his return from Mansfeld and Borna. However, it was not published until early June. In the meantime, in mid-May, a great
defeat had been inflicted on the peasant forces at Frankenhausen.
The slaughter was terrible, and to many people Luther seemed
in his tract to be calling on the victorious princes to beat and
trample an already crushed foe. Luther was, in fact, charged
with being unchristian in his actions, and unscholarly in his
vocabulary. To this point we shall return later.

Then, too, in the midst of the revolt Luther took the rather
important step of marrying Katherine von Bora, an ex-nun. The
marriage was celebrated at the very time when news of the
peasant disasters was being received daily.[9] Criticism became
so strong that even Luther's friends and associates indicated that
some kind of reply should be made to his critics. As a result,
in July, 1525, Luther wrote a third tract entitled, *An Open Letter
Concerning the Harsh Booklet Against the Peasants*.[10] This was
an attempt by Luther to still the critics and also to ask for
mercy for those who had been innocent of wrong-doing in the
war. He asked the princes to spare those who asked for mercy
and for pardon, although he in no way apologized for his second
tract.

The foregoing has been in the nature of a survey of Luther's
actions during the revolt. Now it is necessary to answer, if possible, the question of why he did what he did: Why was Luther
so bitter about the peasants? And why did he advocate such
violent and drastic measures to insure their defeat? In this
connection, it is necessary to examine, rather briefly, three factors: (1) Luther's economic and social status in sixteenth-cen-

tury Saxony, (2) his political theories or ideas on government, and (3) his personal evaluation of what a winning peasantry would mean for his movement and for himself personally.

It must be emphasized, first of all, that Luther was not concerned about his own personal safety. He had amply demonstrated in his appearance before the Diet of Worms and in his early return from the Wartburg that he was a man liberally endowed with personal courage. At Worms he had stood his ground defiantly before the most powerful ecclesiastical nobles of the church. Since Luther had been placed under the imperial ban, his return from the Wartburg also took considerable courage. Luther was indeed not concerned about personal safety. Even his most severe critics have never challenged this aspect of his life. But Luther was afraid—afraid of what might happen to his Movement, afraid of what might happen to his family, and afraid of what might happen to his loyal supporters among the middle classes and the nobility who had done much to aid him and who had given much financial and moral support to his cause of reform.

Let us look, now, at the afore-mentioned three factors which I believe to have been instrumental in determining Luther's position during the revolt. First, Luther's economic and social position must be considered.[11] Many earlier writers on Luther felt that Luther himself was of peasant background; and his critics thus freely attacked Luther's actions during the revolt, saying in effect that he betrayed people of his own kind. Recently, emphasis on Luther's supposed peasant background has diminished. The Reformer, it is now recognized, was a member of the rising middle class in Germany. Researchers have pointed to the records of the University of Erfurt which indicate that Luther came from a family that "had." And it is also pointed out that when Luther became a priest, Hans Luther (Martin's father) journeyed to the monastery with a company of twenty horsemen and gave the Augustinians a gift of twenty *gulden* in celebration of the big event. This was considered a handsome gift, since the price of an ox at the time was usually one or two *gulden*. It has also been established that Martin was born in a two-story house in Eisleben—not the usual dwelling of a peasant of fifteenth-century Germany. Again, research has shown that Hans Luther had done so well in the mining industry in the Mansfeld area that he became the proprietor of several mines with numerous employees. Moreover, he was chosen as a member of the city council, a position reserved only for the most respected and most wealthy of the town's citizens. This honor came before Martin ever entered the university.

Thus, as far as immediate family background is concerned, Luther's parents were members of the middle class and reasonably well off. In looking at his own economic position, especially after his break with Rome, one can say that Luther himself was rather well-to-do also. Although his salary as a professor at Wittenberg was not great, the usual practice was for the Elector of Saxony to supplement this sum with additional grants when the need arose. This was especially true after Luther's marriage. And it has been established that Luther's property holdings and gifts at one time amounted to around 150,000 dollars.[12]

Economically and socially, then, Luther was identified with the middle class and not with the peasantry. It is true that the Luders or Luthers originally were free landholders, and Luther visited members of the clan on his trips to Borna and elsewhere, finding many still engaged in agriculture. But he was a townsman, and had been reared as such. He nevertheless had sympathy for the simple tillers of the soil, as he called them, and naturally was quite upset when the peasant revolt broke out. But in no sense was he a traitor to his class.

In turning to our second consideration, we find that in the realm of politics and political theory Luther believed that government had been ordained by God to rule on earth, to protect the innocent, and to punish the guilty. Throughout his entire career he believed that the greatest sin that a person could commit was to attempt a violent overthrow of government. That is why it is necessary to go back to the Wittenberg Disturbances and the Knights' Revolt to gain an appreciation of Luther's consistency in this matter. Here is what Luther had to say about rebels in his tract, *An Open Letter Concerning the Harsh Booklet Against the Peasants:*[13]

> My little book was not written against simple evil-doers, but against rebels. You must make a very great distinction between a rebel, and a thief, or a murderer, or any other kind of evil-doer. For a murderer, or other evil-doer, leaves the head of the government alone, and attacks only the members of their property; nay, he fears the ruler. So long as the head remains, no one ought to attack such a murderer, because the head can punish him; but everyone ought to await the judgment and command of the head, to whom God has committed the sword and the office of punishment. But a rebel attacks the head himself and interferes with his sword and his office, and therefore his crime is not to be compared with that of a murderer. He cannot wait until the head gives commands and passes judgment, for the head himself is captured and beaten and cannot give them. But everyone who can must run, uncalled and unbidden, and as a true member, must help to rescue his head by thrusting, hewing, and killing, and must risk his life and goods for the sake of the head. . . . Other wicked deeds are single acts; rebellion is a Noah's flood of wickedness.

> I am called a clergyman and have the office of the Word, but if I were the servant even of a Turk and saw my lord in danger I would forget my spiritual office and thrust and hew as long as I had a heartbeat left. If I were slain in so doing, I should go straight to heaven. For rebellion is a crime that deserves no other court nor mercy, whether it be among the heathen, Jews, Turks, Christians, or any other people; it is already heard, judged, condemned, and sentenced to death at anybody's hands. There is nothing to do about it except to kill quickly, and give the rebel his deserts. No murderer does so much evil, and none deserves so much evil. For a murderer commits a penal offense, and lets the penalty stand; but a rebel tries to make wickedness free and unpunishable, and attacks the punishment itself.

Luther considered that the form of government was a matter of human determination, but that government itself, of whatever form, was a divine institution, ordained by God. We may say parenthetically that Luther's writings show his favoring of the monarchial form of government, and especially that of the Holy Roman Empire, a state for which his own prince was one of the electors.

This brings us to our third consideration, it being necessary now to probe a question which Luther must have asked himself during the revolt: What would happen if the peasants were victorious? Luther had had considerable experience with radical leaders. During the Wittenberg Disturbances a few years earlier, he had had to deal with the flamboyant and somewhat peculiar Karlstadt, Zwilling, and the Zwickau prophets. In Wittenberg during Luther's absence they had attempted many reforms or modifications of the church service. In accomplishing these, they had seized property under the control of the town council, and they had destroyed images, altars, vestments, and the like—much to the disgust of Luther when he was informed of their actions. During the peasants' uprising this radical action had been accelerated, and men like Muenzer, Gaismyr, Hipler, and again Karlstadt, had gone far beyond church reform. They had preached social, economic, and political equality. And as far as Luther was concerned, they had distorted his concept of Christian Liberty into an evil, carnal, worldly thing, in which he never believed and which, moreover, he had never taught.

The peasants under their radically inspired leaders had demonstrated not only a disregard for property but also for human life. The atrocity of Weinsberg, in which a castle had been taken and the inhabitants then slaughtered after the truce, was a demonstration of the peasants' evil intent, and proof that they could not be trusted. Luther had considered that the Twelve Articles were a promising start for negotiation. And he had applauded the peasants at that time for their desire to live according to the Gospel and to be guided by the Word of God. In the foreword of these Articles, the peasants had stated that they would change any of the demands if these demands could be shown to be contrary to the Gospel. But after March, 1525, Luther believed that the peasants had demonstrated an unwillingness to listen to anyone. They had certainly refused to abide by his advice.

Luther must have believed that all for which he had fought and struggled would be destroyed if the peasant movement succeeded. Muenzer's social and economic revolution was anathema to him. Then too, in addition to the consequences for his own teaching (we must admit that this was paramount), there were personal economic considerations for Luther the man. He had just married, and had acquired the Black Cloister and other property which had made him one of the wealthy citizens of Wittenberg. His parents were also reasonably well off. He could certainly ask what would happen to his wife, to his family, and to their holdings were the peasants to be successful. By reason of his trips in April and May, and as a result of continued correspondence with individuals throughout the rebellious areas, he recognized that many people of the middle class had suffered in the conflict. Would he be spared if the revolt reached Wittenberg?

Then there was the other side too: What would happen if the princes were victorious? The Elector of Saxony had provided the protection which had allowed Luther's movement to grow strong and to show promise of growing even stronger. Other princes besides the Elector had also already demonstrated their support for this ex-monk. Furthermore, these very individuals were, it must be remembered, the authorities which Luther felt were ordained by God to rule on earth. Any change in the form of government would have to come about through peaceful means. The Reformer admonished the members of his own congregation in 1522 that only through prayer and the Will of God could change come. At that time he said: "Had I desired to foment trouble, I could have brought great bloodshed upon Germany. Yea, I could have started such a little game at Worms that even the emperor would not have been safe. But what would

it have been? A fool's play. I did nothing; I left it to the Word."[14]
In his evaluation and judgment, a princely victory would mean
the continued expansion of the movement, and justice for all.

Now let us examine the criticisms of Luther which arose as
a result of his position during the war. There are four basic ones:
namely, (1) he had used intemperate language in his tracts;
(2) the unfortunate timing of the publication of the three tracts
showed poor judgment on Luther's part; (3) he had given the
peasants cause to believe that he was in favor of their movement,
and then in a sudden shift had gone against them; and (4) his
marriage to Katherine von Bora was an insult to the peasants because of the sweeping victory of the princes at Frankenhausen.

As to the first criticism, if one examines the writings of other
men of letters of the sixteenth century, he will find that Luther
was no better nor worse than his scholarly contemporaries.[15] The
Reformer was no more violent nor intemperate. Concerning
the timing of the tracts, it must be remembered that the word
"war" was really a misnomer, and that there were still peasant
bands fighting after Frankenhausen—a fact of which Luther
was aware. He hoped that his second tract would cause the
remaining rebels to stop. We do know, of course, that Luther
was not deterred by the report of Muenzer's death and the
defeat at Frankenhausen. Though he regretted the heavy
slaughter, he felt that the peasants deserved it.

The third criticism—namely, that he had given the peasants
cause to believe that he was on their side—is completely un-
founded. Nowhere in his voluminous writings on government,
economics, or political theory did he ever deviate from a well-
defined and oft-repeated position concerning rebellion or changes
in government. His great political writings begin in the year 1520,
and from that date to well after 1525 he continued to insist that
government was ordained by God, and that rebellion was the
greatest sin which man could commit against man. Perhaps,
one can say that some of the titles of his works were misleading;
such as, *On Christian Liberty*, and *On Secular Governing—How
Far One Ought to Obey It*. But nowhere in these writings was

there anything remotely concerned with political equality. In the Wittenberg Disturbances he had stopped church reform which had been wrought by force. In the Knights' Revolt he had condemned the Free Imperial Knights of Germany for attacking the Elector of Mainz, one of Luther's greatest enemies. And again in the Peasants' War he advocated change by peaceful means.

His marriage was also criticized for its timing. In June, 1525, a public ceremony was held in Wittenberg. Luther had finally taken the step which he had urged others to take. He was striking another blow in behalf of his beliefs. One may question whether Luther could have prevented a public ceremony and celebration from being held. Had such been possible, criticism might have been reduced; for, as we have already indicated, the marriage came, unfortunately, just after news of the defeat of the peasants at Frankenhausen. But Katherine had, in fact, been living in Wittenberg since 1523; and it is known that as early as May, 1525, Luther intended to marry this young woman.

Actually, then, one can see that Luther's every action could almost have been predicted beforehand. He had always stood for law and order against the forces of disharmony. He had counseled obedience to government regardless of the form of that government and regardless of the masters of that government. Change was not impossible nor undesirable, but such change would have to come through peaceful means. Only through prayer and the Will of God could change be permanent and beneficial to all. Luther was consistent—boringly so. No one who had read any of his tracts on government, economic, or social problems could have misinterpreted Luther's position. No one who had listened to Luther's sermons on these issues could have misunderstood his actions.

NOTES

1. This brief study is based on a paper which the author presented before the Social Science Division of St. Olaf College, in April, 1960.

2. The bibliography on the Peasants' War is too extensive for listing here. But one outstanding work must be mentioned, Günther Franz, *Der deutsche Bauernkrieg* (Munich and Berlin: R. Oldenbourg, 1933), 2 vols. (2nd. ed., Darmstadt: Wissenschaftliche Buchgesellschaft, 1956). This is the definitive work on this subject, and it is indispensable for any study of the period.

3. The study of these three events as influences on Luther's political and economic ideas provided the basis for the author's doctoral dissertation at the University of Michigan directed by Professor Albert Hyma.

4. See Herman Barge, *Andreas Bodenstein von Karlstadt* (Leipzig,, 1905), 2 vols.; and Georg Berbig, *Georg Spalatin und sein Verhaltnis zu Martin Luther auf Grund ihres Briefwechsels bis zum Jahre 1525* (Halle, 1905).

5. Many copies of the Twelve Articles are available. I have consulted Benjamin J. Kidd, *Documents Illustrative of the Continental Reformation* (Oxford, 1911), and the copy in Adolph Spaeth, *et. al.*, eds., *Works of Martin Luther with Introduction and Notes* (Philadelphia, 1915-1932), 6 vols. The latter title hereafter cited as *Works of Martin Luther.*

6. See J. K. F. Knaake, *et. al.*, eds., *D. Martin Luthers Werke, Kritische Gesamtausgabe* (Weimar, 1883-   ), Vol. XVIII, pp. 291-334. Hereafter cited as *Weimar ed.* Extensive quotations with commentary appear in Albert Hyma, *Renaissance to Reformation* (Grand Rapids, Mich., 1950; rev. ed., 1955).

7. This subject has been adequately treated in Ernest G. Schwiebert, *Luther and His Times. The Reformation from a New Perspective* (St. Louis, Mo., 1950).

8. *Works of Martin Luther,* IV, pp. 253-254. For full text see *Weimar ed.,* XVIII, pp. 357-361 and the *Erlangen ed.,* XXIV, pp. 288-294.

9. For Luther's marriage see Albert Hyma, *Martin Luther and the Luther Film of 1953* (Ann Arbor, Mich., 1957), pp. 169-180.

10. *Weimar ed.,* XVIII, pp. 384-401.

11. Professor Albert Hyma has written exhaustively on this subject, especially his *Renaissance to Reformation.*

12. For considerable work along this line we are indebted to Ernest G. Schwiebert. See Schwiebert, *op. cit.,* pp. 104-109, 226-230, 262-268.

13. *Works of Martin Luther,* IV, pp. 276-278. For full text see *Weimar ed.,* XVIII, pp. 384-401, and *Erlangen ed.,* XXIV, pp. 295-319.

14. *Erlangen ed.,* XXIII, pp. 219-220.

15. Such a comparison would require a separate study. These tracts of Luther written on the Peasants' War were not theological treatises, and Luther's choice of words used in them compares not unfavorably with the vocabulary in the non-theological writings of Calvin and Erasmus.

Chapter 2

MARTIN LUTHER AND THE *DEVOTIO MODERNA* IN HERFORD

By WILLIAM M. LANDEEN

(Reprinted from *Dawn of Modern Civilization,* pp. 145-164)

THE problem of the impact of the *Devotio Moderna* on Martin Luther has in recent years received deserved recognition. The first American historian to call attention to the probable influence of Groote's movement on the Wittenberg Reformer was Albert Hyma, who, in his *Christian Renaissance* and later in *The Brethren of the Common Life,*[1] did not hesitate to assert that "the principles of the 'New Devotion' became the spiritual food of many thousands of devout men . . . , and would later . . . be crystallized in the lives of great reformers, like Luther. . . ."[2] That Professor Hyma ascribes to the "New Devotion" a not inconsiderable influence on Luther is clear from this and other statements.

More recently this subject has received special attention by Rudolf Kekow in a doctoral dissertation.[3] Kekow examines the problem with careful, though not exhaustive, investigation and arrives at the conclusion that the *Devotio Moderna* influenced Luther peripherally rather than essentially. It is not possible to establish a connection between the Reformer and the "New Devotion" in his central thinking.[4] And, Karl August Meissinger found that the influence of Groote's movement on Luther was much more passing in character than it was in the case of Erasmus, and added that we meet in Luther's later life with "no trace of a deeper influence. . . ."[5]

But, Luther did know the *Devotio Moderna* not only from his
reading and study but also from considerable personal experience. Various utterances by the Reformer on this subject must
not be passed over too lightly. Scholars in the field could read
with profit E. Barnikol's cogent essay on young Martin's stay
in the Brethren School at Magdeburg.[6] And what shall be said
about the influence on Luther of Gabriel Biel, the last and
most distinguished leader of Groote's movement in Germany,
except that much research remains before adequate conclusions
can be reached on this important question?

As reformer, Luther's personal relationships with the Brethren
of the Common Life in Germany were both strained and pleas-
ant. A case in the former category has recently been investigated
by Kenneth A. Strand in his excellent study *A Reformation
Paradox*, which pictures the Reformer's attack on the Brethren in
Rostock in their attempt to publish a Low-German New Testament.[7] However, at no time in this controversy did Luther attack
the Brethren for their beliefs or religious practices.

The most completely, though by no means fully, documented
relationship of Luther and the Brethren of the Common Life
in Germany is the case of the Brethren House in Herford. Here
we meet the Reformer in correspondence with the Brethren; he
defends their rights in a serious crisis, and he pronounces specifically upon their beliefs and practices. It is our purpose in this
study to assemble the available materials bearing on this interesting and important story.

The beginnings of the Brethren in Herford go back to 1426
when the priest Conrad Westerwold from Osnabrück obtained
a large manor house on the periphery of Herford and proceeded
to install a circle of Brethren who two years later were organized
into a Brethren House. Papal approval came in 1431.[8] Conrad
Westerwold was the first rector and continued to lead the house
as late as 1449, when his name disappears from the sources.
During the fifteenth century the Brethren in Herford were
granted numerous privileges, including exemption from taxes.
The last-named favor aroused the opposition of the townsmen to

the point where the Brethren saw fit to effect a compromise by paying an annual tax of eight groschen. The Sisters of the Common Life entered Herford in 1453 and remained there until their dissolution in 1571. The Brethren remained in Herford until 1841, when the last member of the house died.

The city of Herford came under the influence of Luther's ideas rather early. In 1522, Gerard Kropp, rector of the Augustinians in Herford, began to preach the new doctrines with success. It is plausible to hold that the Brethren and the Sisters in Herford knew about Kropp's activity, but their interest in Luther came from another source; namely, from Jacob Montanus, scholar, humanist, friend of Melanchthon, member of the Brethren House, and Father Confessor to the Sisters of the Common Life in Herford.

Jacob Montanus, also known as Jacob of Spires, came out of the Münster circle of Brethren and humanists. He was a pupil of Alexander Hegius, the famous schoolmaster of Emmerich and Deventer, a schoolmate of John Busch, and a favorite of Rudolph von Langen, whose reform of the cathedral school in Münster made it a famous center of humanistic culture in the early fifteenth century. It was Von Langen who, in or about 1512, sent Jacob Montanus to the Brethren House in Herford to assist the Brethren in their school activities in that city.[9]

Just when and how Jacob Montanus came under Luther's influence escapes us. It must have been before 1523, and the medium could well have been Melanchthon. When the now fragmentary correspondence between Wittenberg and the Brethren in Herford opens with Luther's letter to Montanus on July 26, 1523, there is already a fraternal and well established relationship between this humanist and the Reformer. Wrote Luther:

> Grace and peace. It is true, my best Jacob, that one theme keeps me preoccupied constantly, namely, the grace of Christ. This is the reason which you and all my friends must bear in mind if I do not write at all, or write seldom or briefly.
>
> Concerning your latest communication on the sub-

ject of confession, I believe most assuredly that it is permissible to omit completely a recital of each and every sin. A general confession of sins is sufficient to receive the solace of the Gospel and the remission of sins.

As for the rest, as well as how matters are going with us, the bearer of this letter will inform you. From Flanders we have good news; two of our brothers have been burned in the public square in Brussels for the Word of God and for God's grace in Christ.

Farewell and pray for me a sinning sinner![10]

Such a letter implies not only an established correspondence but also the fact that Montanus was the spokesman for Luther's ideas among the Brethren and Sisters in Herford. In this role he was successful. The adherents of the *Devotio Moderna* in Herford were accepting Luther, and by 1525 both the Brethren and the Sisters of the Common Life had gone over to the Wittenberger. In that year both Gerard Wiscamp, the rector, and Henry Telgte, the prorector of the Brethren House, were imprisoned "as Lutherans and heretics" by Bishop Eric of Paderborn and Osnabrück, and were released only when the Brethren paid the sum of 300 gulden as a fine, and further assured the Bishop that they would pay another 1000 gulden should they ever fall into the same heresy again. Actually, Bishop Eric was suing the Brethren in Herford for this latter sum when his death in 1534 stopped the case.[11]

That Luther fell back on Jacob Montanus during these years of change in Herford seems certain. He says so expressly in his first letter to Gerard Wiscamp, rector of the Brethren House.[12]

Grace and peace. My previous letters have not been sent to you but to Montanus;[13] now I am writing you, my dear Gerard, because I know that you and he are as one heart and mind in the Lord. When you show Montanus these lines thank him and ask that the Brethren pray for me the more solicitously, since their prayers and labor are of first concern to me. And I rejoice to be so well remembered by these pious men.

My commentary on Zechariah is now half finished, being delayed by the state of my health. Likewise, the

Prophets in the vernacular have had to silence their harps because of our dispersion.[14] Ask Jacob to pray for us without ceasing that the fears and rumors of the pest may be stilled by the strong medicine of our Lord Christ, and that we again may be together to finish what we have begun. For the one who stirs up fears and rumors, all to hinder the progress of the Word, is Satan, whom through your prayers Christ will put under our feet. Amen.

Our wives send you thanks for your kind sentiments and gifts. Philip's wife is with him at Jena. Bugenhagen and I, together with our wives, salute you fondly and promise with the Lord's help to follow your advice. My little son also greets you. Farewell in the Lord.[15]

The letter indicates clearly the state of affairs among the Brethren in Herford. Up to this time Jacob Montanus had been the chief spokesman for the Reformer and had actually carried both the Brethren and the Sisters of the Common Life with him in his endeavor. But from this point and on, Gerard Wiscamp, as rector of the house, is recognized as the leader of the Brethren, and Luther is specific in the matter. "You and he" (Montanus), says Luther, "are as one heart and mind in the Lord." It is plausible to hold that Luther had not been fully persuaded until he wrote this letter in response to one which he had received from Rector Gerard, that the Brethren in Herford had genuinely embraced his doctrines. His letter leaves no doubt that he had fully accepted them as his followers.

Luther alluded in the letter to his state of health. Soon after, he passed through a period of intense depression (Anfechtungen) and sickness. Gerard Wiscamp sent him a letter of consolation which elicited the following reply:

Grace and peace. I have received your communication of sympathy, my dear Gerard, with much pleasure and gratitude. Christ will reward you in eternity. In truth, this attack was by far the most severe ever, and although my ailment was not unknown to me from my youth, still so troublesome an attack as this I had not expected. Nevertheless, Christ triumphed, but my life was hanging by a most slender thread. I still commend myself to your prayers and to those of the Brethren. I have now recovered, though, of course, I was not able to effect the cure in my own strength. My blessed Christ, who passed through the depth of despair, blasphemy, and death, will enable us to meet in His kingdom. In the meanwhile we must make sure that we serve Him in word and deed. To be sure, this will not justify us, since we are always unprofitable servants, but our glory is to live in the world for Christ, forgetting our former evil life. As for the remainder, Christ is our life and justification. (Ah, how debasing to the flesh to be thus hid in God!) Now I rejoice that I understand Peter's saying that we must fulfil the experience of suffering, however severe, which will befall the brethren everywhere until the end of the world. Salute our Montanus and all the Brethren.[16]

As was his custom, Luther considered both his physical and mental suffering as part of the great cosmic conflict between Christ and Satan, and Christ had "triumphed." But the Brethren in Herford had contributed to the victory by their prayers and consolations, and Luther was grateful.

The correspondence continues, now in a lighter vein. Rector Gerard had sent the Luther family some lamps, and the Reformer replies in his best humor:

Grace and peace in Christ. We have received with pleasure, my dear Gerard the Lightbearer, your letter and the lamps. So much radiancy of spirit and kindness of heart are shown in sending such a gift that it seems right and proper for me, I know not by what oracle or judgment, to nickname you "Lightbearer."[17] For the light of your radiancy and the warmth of your favor are as conspicuous as is your bodily weakness. And so, my Kathy and I make use of your lamps each and every night, and I only regret that we are at this moment not able to send you anything to keep our memory with you alive. It is the more shame in that I cannot even send you something made of paper, which we ought to be able to do easily. But, as the messengers will tell you, nothing has been published recently, and in the meantime the bookdealers steal your purse, to boot. Nevertheless, without indebtedness I might send some items in a package after or at the time that I go to the booksellers. And I might have sent you Isaiah, recently born in the German language, but the copies were gobbled up so quickly that I do not have one left. I shall send you and Montanus some copies as soon as they are off the press again. Herman of Lippstadt, who has been recommended, I shall use gladly in my study and work whenever there is occasion. My dearest Kathy and little son greet you respectfully. Elizabeth left us to be with Christ,[18] having passed from death to life. The Grace of God be with you.[19]

The letters that have survived from this period continue in the fraternal spirit. Luther cannot find Gerard's latest letter and so does not remember its contents. He sends an autographed copy of one of his writings to a Sister of the Common Life in Herford who had sent him a gift. He would gladly send Gerard certain copies of his books, published at Wittenberg, but does not at the moment have them. He requests Gerard to pray for him and for the cause of Christ everywhere.[20] To Montanus he explains his stand toward Erasmus. He will not enter into further controversy with the humanist regardless of the latter's maledictions. And he sends Montanus some autographed writings.[21]

This happy state of things was not to continue. As has already been observed, Luther's teachings had entered the Augustinian Monastery in Herford as early as 1522. The Franciscans had also joined the new movement, and both Augustinians and Franciscans had been supported in their actions by the Brethren of the Common Life under the influence of Jacob Montanus and Gerard Wiscamp. The first secular church in Herford to become Lutheran was located in the new city. It adopted the new faith in 1530, and about a year later the old city church also became Lutheran.[22]

The city council had, it seems, appointed in 1525 a special

commission of nine citizens to deal with the problems arising
out of the monastic establishments in Herford. By 1532 the commission had decided on the usual secularization. The monasteries
were to cease as such, their inmates must attend the city
churches, partake there of the sacraments, and change their
clothing and habits of life.

The Brethren and the Sisters in Herford refused to comply
and appealed to Luther. They sent him also an "Apology" for
their mode of living and asked him to approve of their statement,
which they would read before the city council. Gerard Wiscamp's
letter is specific.

> Grace and peace. Honorable dear doctor and father
> in Christ. Necessity demands that we send you with
> this letter an "Apology" for our mode of life, which we
> plan to read before the city council on Sunday, February
> 18. Therefore I beg you to examine the statement, and
> if you find in it anything misleading or false to delete
> the same, but to let stand whatever is true before God.
> And kindly state your opinion below (if God impresses
> you to read the "Apology"), together with your signa-
> ture. Give my regards to your dear wife. God bless you.
> January 13, 1532.[23]

The "Apology" or "Lebensgrund"[24] which the Brethren and
the Sisters laid before Luther for endorsement is unique among
Reformation documents because it presents two houses of the
Devotio Moderna, which, though Lutheran in spirit and belief,
were still determined to continue to live as they had begun—in
the common life with all that is included in that concept. The
arguments of the "Apology" are all traditional *Devotio Moderna*
arguments and can be found in the constitutions of the various
houses in Germany and in the Low Countries.

In the first place, appeal is made to Holy Scriptures as the
source of the common life with all its requirements as to labor,
dress, sacraments, and good works in Christ "in whose name we
have been baptized."[25]

Second, the Bible clearly permits in addition to the married state the state of purity, which the Brethren and the Sisters practiced. Historically, this type of life, freely undertaken without binding vows, was found in the schools of the prophets in the Book of Kings, in the Acts of the Apostles, in the school which Mark the Evangelist founded in Alexandria, and in Augustin's life with his clergy.[26]

> Third, we desire that our chartered rights in the municipality of Herford shall be protected, just as the canonical status of the school in Wittenberg was left with its rights and honors.[27] This was also stated by Philip Melanchthon in the "Apology" of the confession of faith by the Christian princes.[28] Both the Old and the New Testaments prove definitely that a house-church such as ours, and a concept, life, and dress such as that of the Brethren of the Common Life have their rights and are approved. For everyone in our brotherhood knows how he must act in his outward behavior and actions, so as to fulfil in our house the admonition of the apostle to walk circumspectly and to practice next to faith words of love and good morals. And as Moses and Christ in both Testaments placed law and gospel together in a spiritual regimen even so must our regimen have its Moses because of the weakness of the flesh. For, where neither fear nor obedience is present, there is neither discipline nor honor. And just as a land must have a law of the land, or a Sachsenspiegel, or imperial law, and a city, city law, so must a house[29] have its house-charter and a house-order based on the Word of God and grounded in love.
>
> Briefly, this is the sum of our house-order. We practice truth and a Christian life as if in the presence of God. In the morning from four o'clock till six we apply ourselves to the Word of God with prayer, the speaking of tongues, and study. At six o'clock, in place of the mass, we have exegesis and exposition based on the Holy Scriptures. For the rest of the day everyone has his work to perform. Sundays and evangelical feast days we hold the Lord's Supper as instituted by Christ. In all our conduct and mode of life we walk as if Christ

himself were walking with us in His person. Among other things we operate a school in our house. . . .[30]

The "Apology" ended with the affirmation that everybody in Herford, and especially the Lutheran pastors, knew what the Brethren had believed and suffered, and why their request should be honored.

Luther had been asked to endorse the "Apology," if he could. He responded without reservation:

I, Martin Luther, confess over this my signature that I find nothing unchristian in this statement. Would to God that all monasteries might teach and practice God's word so earnestly.

In returning the "Apology" with his endorsement to Jacob Montanus and Gerard Wiscamp, he wrote almost with abandon:

Grace and peace. I have received your communications and have written about this matter to the senate of your city and asked that your house might be protected and spared the uncertainty which the agitators[31] are occasioning you. As for your mode of life, whensoever you teach pure doctrine and live according to the Gospel of Christ, I am greatly pleased. And oh that the monasteries had been or were today so excellent. I scarcely dare wish so much, for if all were thus, the Church would be blessed overmuch in this life. Your manner of dress and other laudable practices have not hurt the Gospel; rather these old usages serve, once the Gospel is firmly planted, to keep under control the raging,[32] licentious, and undisciplined spirits which today are bent upon destroying, not building. Stand, therefore, in your state, and under this manner of life propagate richly the Gospel, which, indeed, you are doing. Live well and pray for me.[33]

The same day Luther sent the city council in Herford a letter most explicit in its language:

Grace and peace in Christ. Honorable, wise, esteemed Lordships! It has come to my attention that some would force the Sisters and Brethren to give up their manner of life and their dress, and live hereafter according to the formula of the parish priest and of the pastor.[34] However, you know undoubtedly that unnecessary changes, especially in sacred matters, are very dangerous in that hearts and consciences are moved without conviction, when all should serve and work for peace and quietude. Since the Brethren and the Sisters, who were the first among you to receive the Gospel, lead upright lives and conduct an honorable and well-ordered community, and also teach and practice faithfully the true Word, it is my friendly wish that your Lordships will not permit them to experience unrest and disappointments in this matter, but that they be permitted to use clerical garb and practice ancient usages when these do not contravene the Gospel. For such monasteries and Brethren Houses please me beyond measure. And would to God that all monasteries were like these, for then would all parishes, cities, and lands be well served and advised. Pardon me, but your Lordships will know how to deal wisely and according to Christ in this matter, so that neither the pastor nor the parish will suffer but rather gain and improve. I commend you to the Lord. Dated Wittenberg, January 31, 1532.[35]

This is Martin Luther, the destroyer of monasticism, defending and praising quasi-monastic practices. Why did he do this? Was it because of his friendship with Jacob Montanus, who had been his firm supporter in Herford for years and who had as humanist, scholar, teacher, and confessor to the Sisters helped so much in making these houses "the first among you to receive the Gospel"?

We may not err in making this factor a reason for Luther's support, but surely it was not decisive. Luther's reason is explicit: "For such monasteries and Brethren Houses please me beyond measure. And would to God that all monasteries were like these. . . ." And the Brethren he admonished: "Stand, therefore, in your state, and under this manner of life propagate richly the Gospel, which, indeed, you are doing." This was the Reformer's argument for endorsing the *Devotio Moderna* in Herford. That he understood full well what he was doing is inescapable. He had had dealings with the *Devotio Moderna* from his youth and up, and he knew the principles and aims of Groote's movement, as is shown by his correspondence with the Brethren and the city authorities in Herford.

In his letter to the Brethren, Luther had strong language for those who were disturbing them. He called his own pastors in Herford "agitators" and then went on to speak about "raging, licentious, and undisciplined spirits . . . bent upon destroying, not building." While this was scarcely complimentary speech concerning his own followers, it seems to indicate how essentially conservative was Martin Luther. Ancient usages, vows, clerical garb are not barred provided they do not contravene the pure Gospel. Peace and quietude are more important than changes forced upon those whose hearts are not moved by reason. The gospel is not necessarily outward change but inward peace.

What effect did Luther's intervention have upon events in Herford?

That his endorsement of the "Apology" of the Brethren and Sisters and his letter to the city council had blocked the plans to secularize the two houses, is certain. Doctor John Dreyer, the Lutheran pastor in the city church, complained bitterly to the prior of the Brethren House over his loss of face and prestige. This led Gerard Wiscamp, in an unguarded moment, to show Pastor Dreyer Luther's personal letter of January 31 to the Brethren. Infuriated by Luther's statements concerning himself and his fellow pastors, Dreyer now began a systematic campaign of slander, vilification, and falsification against the Brethren and the Sisters, which probably did not stop until the Lutheran leader moved to the city of Minden in 1540.

Again the Brethren appealed to Luther. Again they explained carefully the charges made against them and told how no efforts were spared to malign them on their manner of life even to the inciting of drunken men to stir up feeling against the houses. The schoolwork of the Brethren, always aimed especially at helping poor boys, was now equated with the monastic schools. Their unmarried status was attacked as contrary to the Gospel. Their legal rights to exist were called in question.[36]

The Brethren fought back. They now showed their "Apology," with Luther's approval, to Anna von Limburg, Abbess of Herford, and asked for help and protection. The Abbess took up their cause and arranged for a legal hearing of the case, only to find that the pastors were countering by sending a delegation to Luther to prevent further hearings. She appealed to the Reformer to trust the Brethren completely.[37]

In his reply to the Abbess, Luther recounted his earlier efforts to aid the Brethren. He reiterated their rights to have their own pastoral care and to hold their own services, and asked the Abbess to act as peacemaker for both sides.[38]

Luther also wrote the Commission of Nine in Herford, which had been appointed by the city council to deal with problems arising between monastic establishments and the city during the period of confessional changes. The Commission had written Luther and had also sent a delegation to him—no doubt, to ascertain his attitude in these matters. The most difficult aspect of the Brethren problem was their insistence on continuing their own pastoral care with all the privileges incident to this right. The Lutheran pastors argued that if the Brethren were permitted this privilege, any citizen in Herford could demand the same right, which, if granted, would result in religious chaos.

Luther was explicit:

> . . . however, when the Brethren desire to retain their own church services and do not in their own interests attend your services, it is our judgment that you should in no way pressure or force them to give up theirs so long as they do not conduct them contrary to the Gospel. For one thing is clear: they do hold the right to have their own pastors, a right which is very common in any city. It does not follow from this, however, that every citizen may employ a pastor in his own household.

That is not permitted. This is the important difference
between a common and public assembly and a family
assembly; namely, that what a citizen does in his home
is considered as being done secretly.

Further, you know, as men of understanding, that
there should be no interference in matters that lie outside of our jurisdiction. The Brethren are not under your
jurisdiction, and so you cannot push or force them into
line. This is our advice and request, as you will kindly
understand. Therefore, we ask you to consider that time
will find its own counsel in this matter. They are old,
honorable persons whom we should spare, and as men
of understanding we should not permit anyone to practice malice toward them, for God has individuals among
them who are His.[39]

Both Luther and Melanchthon signed this communication
and sent a copy of it to the Brethren. In a separate letter to
Gerard Wiscamp, Luther counsels mildly that the Brethren
might yield their right of pastoral care but that if they do not
so incline, he will not criticize them.

Therefore, if you desire to retain your parish rights
we do not disapprove. As for your garb, the possessions
of the monastery, and your entire economy, we pro-
nounce that they are altogether under your control.
The city has no authority over you.[40]

The energetic intervention by the Wittenberg reformers
stopped, for the time being, the efforts of the Lutheran pastors
and the city council to limit the activities and rights of the
Brethren. Luther was able to write Gerard Wiscamp:

I am glad, my Gerard, that the racket among you
which Satan started, is sleeping. Christ be praised, who
will establish His peace and cause it to increase. . . .[41]

However, the Brethren were still disturbed over their situation. Especially were they concerned about Luther's statement
in his letter to the Commission of Nine that "time will find its
own counsel." Could this mean that Luther actually would like
to see the Brethren House die out for lack of new members who

were willing to consecrate themselves to a life of virginity and purity? Gerard Wiscamp besought Luther for an explanation of the statement.[42]

Melanchthon replied for Luther, who was still indisposed. He sought to quiet the minds of the Brethren but did not explain Luther's statement.[43] This caused the Brethren to renew their request for an explanation. They "were greatly disturbed" over the assertion and asked Luther and Melanchthon to clarify its meaning.[44]

In their "Apology," sent earlier to Luther, the Brethren had written:

> In order to stand in the liberty which Christ has given us, we do not take [binding] vows, but we retain our freedom, as Christ also forced no one to remain at the time when disciples were leaving Him (John 6:[66]).[45]

The practice of non-binding vows was the very essence of the *Devotio Moderna* as an organized movement. The Brethren were not monks but desired to live lives of purity in the world without vows, which was the Biblical custom, they reasoned. If Luther's statement in any way impinged upon this mode of life, it struck at their future existence.

In a letter dated January 6, 1534, Gerard Wiscamp returns to this point and in so doing restates the whole philosophy of Brethren life.

> We have no other aim than that our life shall be free in Christ, as was at first ordained by our fathers, who 100 years ago stated clearly in writing: "We will not accept vows from anyone, were he even to insist upon them." Our life is meaningful when we can train our own members, which we have done often from our small numbers, to be preachers of God's Word. But, for this office our entire house does not now, so far as I know, have one qualified member, apart from some boys who are scarcely more than children. What will happen eventually? We would like to dedicate ourselves to this task [the training of preachers] permanently. You see,

therefore, how you can support us by your confidence because we seek not our own good in this matter but God's. . . .[46]

It seems that Luther delayed his reply to Gerard's letter. In the meantime the Brethren were encountering new difficulties. The city school in Herford was languishing, and the senate was pressing the Brethren to take it over and to use their building for it. This they did not have the teaching force to do, and they did not want to engage teachers outside of their own ranks. Jacob Montanus died in the course of this year, and no one could take his place as a pedagog. The Brethren, therefore, raised serious objections against assuming new teaching responsibilities, which in turn brought on them fresh attacks both from the Catholic and the Lutheran sides. Again they appealed to Luther to explain himself and to succor them. They declared their readiness to train young boys, as they always had done, to live lives of purity without vows and to become evangelists in their cause. "May the Lord give us good advice through you," they appealed to Luther and Melanchthon.[47]

Again the Reformer took up their cause with the senate in Herford. Again he repeated his earlier opinions concerning these adherents of the *Devotio Moderna.* The Brethren and the Sisters had indeed laid aside the papal yoke and were living in Christian freedom even though they retained their old garb and ancient customs. They lived pious and disciplined lives and worked with their hands as did the Apostle (Paul).[48]

> . . . I could wish that such people were, as God would give His grace, numerous, since they are not dangerous but useful because they are adherents of the Gospel.
> I hear also that they should be burdened with the public school office and its care, although they were never founded for this purpose nor do they receive tax support for this work. Other foundations and monasteries do and should perform this service, but it is not right that these should use what they earn themselves, and are not paid, for such a purpose. . . .

I have written you earlier that the "time would find its own counsel." Now I hear that this is interpreted to mean that they should be forced to comply, although these words meant that time would tell whether they would remain [as they were] or would change of their own free will. I pray your Lordships for Christ's sake to help that no reason is given to speak evil of the Gospel. . . .[49]

Luther sent to Gerard Wiscamp a copy of his communication to the city senate. In the covering letter he again expressed concern that the Brethren and the Sisters were troubled by "the hypocrites of the new Gospel," and he reiterated earlier statements approving their manner of life and organization. They should not be disturbed with public functions such as teaching; other institutions or monasteries could assume that task. And his last extant letter to the men and women of the *Devotio Moderna* in Herford closes with this wish:

I desire exceedingly that your mode of life may be preserved so that in the liberty and grace of Christ you can serve and be useful greatly in love. Salute all your Brethren and Sisters in Christ![50]

Luther's intervention stilled the tumult for the time being. In 1537 it broke out again, only to be quieted once more by the efforts of Luther and Melanchthon. Two years later the Lutheran pastors seem to have made a special effort to destroy the Brethren and the Sisters, and it was not until 1542 that their houses were finally allowed to remain. Again it was Luther's and Melanchthon's advice that prevailed.[51] However, by then Doctor John Dreyer, the fighting Lutheran reformer of Herford, had gone to Minden,[52] and Gerard Wiscamp, the stubborn defender of the *Devotio Moderna* in Herford, had gone to his rest.[53]

Luther's part in the more than decade-long struggle was difficult but honorable. He criticized his own pastors consistently and, at moments, sharply, while to the city authorities he was courteous but firm. He sought constantly to transfer the conflict from the utilitarian plane of secularization to the higher plane of liberty in Christ to retain old customs and ways of living as long as these advanced the Gospel. That he understood and valued the aims of the Brethren and the Sisters in Herford is clear from his several pronouncements. The entire episode reveals how many-sided the Wittenberg reformer could really be. Throughout, Luther was the defender of the weak, the counsellor of both the weak and the strong, and the advocate of compromise in the interests of peace.[54]

NOTES

1. A. Hyma, *The Christian Renaissance* (Grand Rapids, 1924); *The Brethren of Common Life* (Grand Rapids, 1950).

2. *The Christian Renaissance*, 156-157.

3. R. Kekow, *Luther und die Devotio Moderna* (Düsseldorf, 1937).

4. Kekow, *op. cit.*, 18.

5. K. A. Meissinger, *Der katholische Luther* (Munich, 1952), 24.

6. E. Barnikol, "Martin Luther in Magdeburg und die dortige Brüder-schule," in *Theologische Arbeiten* (Tübingen, 1917), 1-62.

7. K. A. Strand, *A Reformation Paradox* (Ann Arbor, 1960).

8. L. Hölscher, "Geschichte des Gymnasiums zu Herford I," in *Program des Friedrichs Gymnasium zu Herford 1869*. The Statutes of the house were published in *Theologische Monatschrift*, Vol. II (Mainz, 1851), 543-582.

9. J. B. Nordhoff, *Denkwürdigkeiten aus dem Münsterischen Humanismus* (Münster, 1874), 93, 123.

10. *W. A. Br.* III, 117. Additional light on the Herford Brethren has recently been shed by Robert Stupperich in "Luther und das Fraterhaus in Herford," in *Geist und Geschichte der Reformation. Festgabe Hanns Rückert* (Berlin, 1966), pp. 219-238.

11. The Brethren argued that their promise to pay 1000 gulden had been forced on them and was therefore invalid. See *W. A. Br.* IV, 244, and L. Hölscher, *Reformationsgeschichte der Stadt Herford* (Herford, 1888), 16.

12. That Luther and Montanus exchanged letters during these years is further substantiated by a letter from Montanus to Willibald Pirckheimer, dated April 23, 1526, in which he asks Pirckheimer "to return the letters to Luther and Melanchthon which, I believe, you have." Perhaps Montanus had sent the Nuremberg humanist copies of these letters and now wanted them returned. See *W. A. Br.* III, 117.

13. The editors of Luther's correspondence say (*W. A. Br.* IV, 244) that Gerard Wiscamp became rector in 1528. This cannot be correct. He was imprisoned with his prorector in 1525 as responsible for the heresy of all the Brethren in his house and was held responsible ever after. Further, Luther's letter to him on September 2, 1527, is plainly written to him as rector.

14. The pest in and about Wittenberg had caused many students and professors to flee to the University of Jena.

15. *W. A. Br.* IV, 243, 244, September 2, 1527.

16. *W. A. Br.* IV, 319, 320, January 1, 1528. Luther's illness fell in October, and Wiscamp's letter of sympathy was probably written in November, 1527.

17. Or, "Lampstand."

18. Born December 10, 1527; died August 3, 1528.

19. *W. A. Br.* IV, 584, 585, October 20, 1528.

20. *W. A. Br.* V, 87, May 28, 1529.

21. *W. A. Br.* V, 88, May 28, 1529.

22. The principal agent in winning these churches was John Dreyer, an Augustinian monk in Herford. He became in 1532 the first Lutheran pastor in Herford and drew up an excellent church order for the city.

23. *W. A. Br.* VI, 248, 249.

24. Published by Baxmann, in *Zeitschrift für historische Theologie,* 1861, 632-634.

25. *Ibid.,* 632.

26. *Ibid.,* 632, 633.

27. The reference is to the University of Wittenberg, which retained its privileges when it became Lutheran.

28. Probably refers to the Augsburg Confession of Faith and incidental writings therewith by Melanchthon.

29. The emphasis is on a Brethren House as distinguished from a monastery.

30. Baxmann, *op. cit.,* 633. The last sentence of this paragraph was not completed. That the Brethren had operated a school in Herford for decades seems certain.

31. . . . *Clamatores; i.e.,* John Dreyer and Henry Vogelmann, Lutheran pastors in Herford.

32. . . . *imo [in] genito euangelio multum iuvant contra furiosos.* . . .

33. *W. A. Br.* VI, 255, 256, January 31, 1532.

34. As in note 31.

35. *W. A. Br.* VI, 254, 255. Luther was ill and could only sign the letter written by an amanuensis.

36. *W. A. Br.* VI, 290-293, April 13, 1532, Gerard Wiscamp to Martin Luther.

37. *W. A. Br.* VI, 293, 294, April 14, 1532. Anna von Limburg was styled "Abbess in the diocese of Paderborn."

38. *W. A. Br.* VI, 300, April 22, 1532. Melanchthon wrote the letter for Luther, who was ill.

39. *W. A. Br.* VI, 296, 297, April 22, 1532.

40. *W. A. Br.* VI, 298, April 22, 1532. Melanchthon wrote the letter for Luther.

41. *W. A. Br.* VI, 380, October 19, 1532.

42. *W. A. Br.* VI, 473, June 5, 1533.

43. *W. A. Br.* VI, 472, July 4, 1533. Gives Melanchthon's answer.

44. *W. A. Br.* VI, 535, October 10, 1533.

45. See Baxmann, *op. cit.,* 634.

46. *W. A. Br.* VII, 7, 8, January 6, 1534.

47. *W. A. Br.* VII, 106-108, October 9, 1534.

48. I Thess. 4:11; II Thess. 3:12; Acts 18:3.

49. *W. A. Br.* VII, 113, 114, October 24, 1534.

50. *W. A. Br.* VII, 114, 115, October 24, 1534.

51. *W. A. Br.* VII, 112, 113, gives a summary of these events.

52. In 1540. His leaving Herford may have been occasioned by his implacable attitude toward the Brethren.

53. Also in 1540. It was his successor in Herford who helped settle the issue, just as did the successors of John Dreyer.

54. That the Brethren in Herford returned to Catholicism cannot be established from the sources.

Chapter 3

LUTHER'S CONDEMNATION OF THE ROSTOCK NEW TESTAMENT

By Kenneth A. Strand

(Reprinted in shortened form from *Andrews University Seminary Studies,* I [1963], 108-120)

I T may seem paradoxical that Martin Luther, champion of the cause for the vernacular Bible, should have condemned a German Bible translation of his day. Yet this is precisely what occurred late in 1529 as the Reformer initiated a chain of correspondence which led to the interruption and cutting short of work on a New Testament being produced by the Brethren of the Common Life at Rostock. Luther's efforts to suppress this publication were so successful that its extant representations are few indeed. Only four nearly complete copies, plus some additional fragments, are known to us .[1]

Before we turn our attention to the historical circumstances surrounding the printing and condemnation of this Rostock New Testament, it will be well to give a brief description of the work itself. The publication is an octavo edition. The print of its main text is roughly comparable to what we call "pica," while that used for glosses and other additions is slightly smaller. There is profuse marginal space, but much of this is taken up with various kinds of notes. The Biblical text itself, from Matthew through the Book of Acts, where the publication ends, is given on the recto and verso of leaves numbered from 1 to 248. In addition, there are some sixteen preliminary leaves.

The page style of the Brethren's Testament is as follows: The main, central portion of the page is devoted to the presentation of the Low-German translation of the Biblical text. Interspersed with the text are notations designated as "glosses," and at the beginnings of the chapters are other notations called "summaries." The page margins toward the binding edge contain capital letters as paragraph indicators, and the outer margins contain such items as scriptural cross-references, notations of Luther's renderings, and references to the Church Year.

We must now ask, Who were these Brethren of the Common Life at Rostock—the publishers of this New Testament—, and why did Luther condemn their Bible translation?

The Rostock Brethren of the Common Life were part of a significant spiritual and intellectual movement known as the "Devotio Moderna." This movement, a reform movement within the Roman Catholic communion, had originated in the Low Countries toward the end of the fourteenth century, and from thence had spread into Germany during the fifteenth century. The Brethren house at Rostock had its beginnings in the year 1462 when three Brothers from Münster arrived in Rostock and began to live the Common Life there. This Rostock establishment of the Brethren came soon to be known as the "House at the Green Garden," and its members derived somewhat later the name "Michaelisbrüder."[2]

About the year 1475 these Brethren of the Common Life at Rostock instituted a printing press at their establishment.[3] It is interesting to notice that a large number of the works issuing from this press during its operation under the auspices of the Brethren—that is, from about 1475 to 1532—were in the vernacular. Most of these works were in German, but some were in Danish. [4]

The pioneer leaders of the "Devotio Moderna" had favored and encouraged the use of the vernacular. Gerard Groote (d. 1384), the founder of the movement, translated portions of Scripture into his native Dutch language,[5] and Gerard Zerbolt of Zutphen (d. 1398), an early writer for the Brethren of the Common Life, went so far as to produce a book in which he presented reasons why laymen should have the Bible in the vernacular. [6] In view of such facts, it is hardly strange that the Catholic Brothers at Rostock should undertake to publish a Low-German edition of the New Testament.

Luther's opposition to the Brethren's Testament was evidently caused neither by objection to the language used, for he himself favored use of the vernacular, nor by opposition to the Brethren themselves, for the Reformer evidenced a favorable attitude toward the Brotherhood of the Common Life. In January of 1532, for example, he came to the defense of the Brethren at Herford when these were involved in difficulties with the Protestant city authorities there. [*] And it must also be remembered that Luther himself had spent one year of his youth with the Brethren of the Common Life at Magdeburg, and so had been able to obtain first-hand knowledge about their manner of life and their piety. Apparently his first contact with the Brethren had left a lasting and favorable impression upon him.

The true basis for Luther's opposition to the New Testament which was being produced by the Brethren of the Common Life at Rostock is revealed in two letters he penned in November of 1529. The first, dated on the 23rd of that month, was a request made to his own prince, the Elector John of Saxony. [7] In this letter, Luther stated that according to word he had received from several pious burghers of Lübeck some "Loll-brothers" at Rostock were in the process of printing a Saxon translation of Jerome Emser's Testament. For his own part, he could tolerate the text of Emser's publication, for it was essentially the Reformer's own translation. However, this Emserian Testament had been so knavishly poisoned with Emser's glosses and annotations that it could bear no fruit, but do only harm. Luther's request therefore to the Elector was that the latter would make intercession with Duke Henry of Mecklenburg, one of the rulers of the Duchy in which Rostock was located. [8]

Upon receiving word from John's counsellors that the Elector was away, Luther hastily prepared the second letter of which we have spoken. This was addressed directly to Duke Henry, and bore the date of November 27. [9] In it Luther repeated the information sent to John, and besought Henry to honor the Gospel of Christ and to rescue all souls as

[*] See above: William M. Landeen's chapter, pp. 45-64; also an allusion in Hyma's Introduction, p. 15.

far as possible by not allowing the printing of the Brethren's New Testament.

Thus, Luther's objection to the Brethren's project was based on his having heard that they were printing Jerome Emser's version. But the offensive portion was not so much Emser's rendition of the Biblical text as it was the glosses and other additions.

Though Luther had not himself seen the Brethren's translation (as evidenced from the correspondence itself), the report he had received seems to have been quite accurate. The very title-page of their Low-German Testament announces it to be "The New Testament as translated into German by the Highly Learned Jerome Emser . . . ." And the contents indicate the same, both as to the text itself and as to the other items included. Moreover, the page style of the Brethren's work is strikingly similar to that of the 1528 and 1529 Leipzig editions of Emser's version. [10]

But just who was this Jerome Emser and what can we say of his New Testament? [11] Emser, a Swabian nobleman, was at the time of the publication of the first edition of his Testament, in August of 1527, a private secretary and commissioner for Duke George of Albertine Saxony, in whose service he had been since 1505. His earlier education had been acquired at Tübingen, Basel and Leipzig, and he had taught for a short while at Erfurt, where he claimed to have had Luther as a student. [12] After the Leipzig Disputation of June 27 to July 16, 1519, a fiery literary feud developed between Emser and Luther. And when the latter issued his "September Testament" of 1522, Emser hastened (in 1523) to publish a detailed and incisive critique of it. [13] Then some four years later Emser issued his own rival New Testament. [14] A comparison of this Testament with Luther's reveals that Emser simply revised Luther's text, often with the obvious purpose of bringing certain of the Lutheran readings into harmony with the Vulgate and with Catholic interpretation of Scripture. [15]

The glosses in the Emserian publication were of quite

another stamp, however. Though a number of these were historical explanations and the like—and thus must have been innocuous even from Luther's point of view—, others were critical of the Reformer and his teachings. For example, Emser's gloss following[16] Mt 3:2 includes the words, "Take heed for the heretics, who despise penance and confession." Then a few verses further along, another gloss draws an analogy between the Jews boasting of Abraham and the "heretics" of Christ. In the next chapter a gloss following verse 6 states that "here the devil leaves out a part of the Scripture, taking only what serves him, as his sons the heretics also do." And in a gloss following Mt 7:20, we read that "every heretic is a bad tree, which brings no good fruit." Such glosses must have seemed to the Reformer somewhat like a running commentary directed against the Reformation.

In addition to the glosses, some of the marginal notations may have been offensive to Luther too, especially the ones which pointed in a critical tone to his renditions of Scripture. Furthermore, in the rather popular 1529 Cologne edition of the Emserian New Testament there were lengthy sections of critical material bearing the designation "annotations." These appeared at the end of various Bible chapters and represented excerpts from the second edition of Emser's critique of Luther's version.

It is possible that the Reformer may have had these "annotations" in mind as he penned his letters to Elector John and Duke Henry in November of 1529, for those letters specifically mention "annotations." But if this was the case, the Brethren's Testament must have been somewhat less objectionable than Luther had expected it to be, for the Brethren did not incorporate these particular extended critical notes in their edition. They did, however, present notations of Lutheran readings, and references to the places in the Emserian critique where such readings were challenged. Moreover, they did little or nothing to ameliorate the anti-Lutheran, anti-Reformation glosses.

Luther's letter to the Reformation-minded Duke Henry brought quick results. On December 18, the very day on which Henry received the Reformer's letter, the Duke sent a dispatch to the Rostock city council.[17] In this communication he spoke of the Brethren's New Testament as "objectionable" and "not allowable." And he requested that the council would, with the threat of penalties, bring about the cessation of the Brethren's printing of the said Testament and also recall any copies which might already have been circulated. The council, itself favorable to the Reformation and under the influence of the strongly Protestant syndic John Oldendorp, took action forbidding the Brethren's project.

The Brethren did not give up easily, however. Their printer John Holt visited the court of Duke Albert VII of Mecklenburg, who was more Catholic-minded than was Henry.[18] Holt's trip, though apparently unproductive of tangible aid, must at least have given the Brethren moral support for the continuation of their undertaking. In any event, they decided to proceed—secretly—with their project. What the precise schedule of their printing was we do not know. Nor do we know the exact chronology of the delay or delays which they encountered. It does seem likely, however, that their partially completed New Testament did not issue from the press until early in 1532.[19] The final termination of their project appears to have been brought on by the city council's taking action against Holt, the printer, and Martin Hilleman, the rector of the Rostock Brethren house. These men were arrested because of their manifest non-compliance with the council's earlier restraining order. They were able to secure their release only by swearing loyalty to the council, as the document containing their declaration indicates.[20]

Though the Brethren's New Testament was based primarily on the Emserian version, both as to text and glosses, an interesting fact is that the Brethren also used other German versions. Among these were a Low-German translation of

Luther's New Testament, the Lübeck Bible of 1494 and possibly other sources.[21]

While it may not seem strange that the Brethren should use the Lübeck Bible and other Catholic versions, how can we account for their use of a Lutheran version?

Perhaps the most we can say regarding the reason for the Brethren's use of a Lutheran New Testament is that in all likelihood some of the Rostock Brothers were at this time friendly to the Reformation forces.   This was not the case, of course, with Hilleman, who showed a definitely hostile and non-cooperative attitude toward the city council. But a later rector, Henricus Arsenius, manifested a friendly spirit toward the Reformation party,[22] and it may be that other Brothers with similar sentiments were already members of the "House at the Green Garden" at the time when work was begun on the Low-German Emserian Testament. If such were the case, we could well expect these Reformation-minded Brothers to have been responsible for securing the use of Luther's New Testament in the preparation of the Rostock translation. [23]

But we must take care, on the other hand, not to over-emphasize the Brethren's use of a Lutheran New Testament. For even though they did revise a strikingly large number of the Emserian readings on the basis of the Lutheran version, their Testament was still definitely "Emserian." This is true of the text itself as a whole, especially in points where Emser had criticized Luther's rendition. It is also true of the glosses and other additions. The Brethren consistently adopted glosses of the type to which we have already made reference, regardless of how injurious these may have been to Luther and the Reformation interests. For the Brethren, as for their Emserian prototype, the "heretics" constituted an evil tree, were the devil's "sons" or "children," [24] and so forth.

This modified anti-Lutheran publication failed, however, to accomplish its manifest purpose; namely, to counteract Luther's New Testament in the Low-German-speaking area in and around Rostock. For as we have already seen, Luther's influence and activity brought the Brethren's work to premature termination, followed by confiscation and destruction. Then came silence and well-nigh oblivion—silence and oblivion almost unbroken until nineteenth-century discoveries began to bring to light the scant remains now in evidence of this intriguing Reformation-era vernacular Bible edition.

NOTES

[1] Three of the nearly complete copies are in Germany: at the State Library in Stuttgart, the University Library in Rostock, and the State Library in Schwerin. The fourth copy is in America, at the Harper Library of the University of Chicago. Regarding locations of the copies in Germany, as well as the fragments, see Carl Meltz, "Die Drucke der Michaelisbrüder zu Rostock 1476 bis 1530," in *Wissenschaftliche Zeitschrift der Universität Rostock*, V (1955-56), 246, 247; and Conrad Borchling and Bruno Claussen, comps., *Niederdeutsche Bibliographie* (Neumünster, 1931-36), No. 1059 (I, col. 473). Selections from the Lemgo fragments have been published in Ernst Weissbrodt, *Das niederdeutsche Neue Testament nach Emsers Übersetzung Rostock 1530* (Bonn, 1912). An Introduction on p. 2 of this work furnishes some information about other fragments as well.

[2] A comprehensive treatment of the Devotio Moderna in Germany has been presented by William M. Landeen, *The Devotio Moderna in Germany in the Fifteenth Century: A Study of the Brethren of the Common Life* (Ph. D. Dissertation, University of Michigan, 1939). Landeen has published the results of this and further research in a series of articles in *Research Studies of the State College of Washington* (hereafter cited as *RSSCW*). The portion of this series dealing with the Rostock Brethren house is "The Devotio Moderna in Germany (Part IV)," *RSSCW*, XXII (1954), 57-71. This section represents material not presented in the original study.

[3] The authoritative treatment concerning this press is Meltz, *op. cit.* The work of Meltz supersedes that of all earlier investigators, including Lisch and Hofmeister, and corrects in many places the results achieved by them.

[4] See esp. the listing given in *ibid.*, pp. 243-247. Of the 32 16th-century works noted there as having been printed by the Brethren (this means omission of Nos. 31 and 57-60), about two-thirds were entirely or partly in Low German. And five other of these publications were in Danish.

[5] See, *e.g.*, Albert Hyma, "Een Vergeten Werk van Geert Groote," in *Nederlandsch Archief voor Kerkgeschiedenis*, XL (1954), 87-95; and Willem Moll, *Geert Groote's Dietsche Vertalingen* (Amsterdam, 1880), pp. 53-77. In the last-mentioned work, note also pp. 78-115, and the introductory discussion on pp. 1-49.

[6] See Albert Hyma, "The 'De Libris Teutonicalibus' by Gerard Zerbolt of Zutphen," in *Nederlandsch Archief voor Kerkgeschiedenis*, XVII (1924), 42-70; also Hyma, *Renaissance to Reformation* (Grand Rapids, Mich., 1951), pp. 578-580.

[7] See Weimar ed., *Briefwechsel*, V, pp. 183, 184. The entry is No. 1497.

[8] The two dukes of Mecklenburg at this time were Henry V and Albert VII.

[9] See Weimar ed., *Briefwechsel*, V, pp. 187, 188. The entry is No. 1499.

[10] These editions, both of which were published by V. Schuman, have glosses interspersed with the Biblical text, use chapter summaries, and contain marginal references to the Church Year calendar and to Luther's rendition. In these respects these publications and the Brethren's Testament are precisely alike. On the other hand, the first Emserian edition, published in 1527 by W. Stöckel at Dresden, has its glosses in the margins and lacks both the chapter summaries and the marginal notations referring to the Church Year and to Luther's rendition. Some other High-German editions published in 1529 by H. Fuchs in Cologne and by J. Fabrum (Faber) in Freiburg i. B. are more similar to the Leipzig editions and to the Brethren's Testament. But here there is notable dissimilarity as well, inasmuch as the Cologne edition contains lengthy "annotations" at the end of its Bible chapters, and the Freiburg publication has its glosses in a sort of appendix at the end of the work.

[11] On the career of Jerome Emser, see esp. Gustav Kawerau, "Hieronymus Emser," in *Schriften des Vereins für Reformationsgeschichte*, No. 61 (Halle, 1898), 1-110.

[12] Most of Emser's work toward the Baccalaureate was done in Tübingen, where he had matriculated in July, 1493. He actually took his Bachelor's examination, however, in Basel, in the winter semester of 1497. At Basel he also earned a Master's degree, in 1499. At the University of Leipzig he pursued studies in the theological field, being awarded a Bachelor's degree in the theological faculty in January, 1505. His brief period of teaching at the University of Erfurt was during the summer semester of 1504, and his claim to have had Luther as a student was made in his *Hieronymi Emsers Quadruplica auff Luters Jungst gethane antwurt/sein reformation belangend* (Leipzig, 1521), fol. Giii, verso. It has been republished in Ludwig Enders, *Luther und Emser* (Halle a. S., 1890, 1892), II, 179.

[13] The first edition of this critique was published by Wolfgang Stöckel in Leipzig in September, 1523. It bore the following title: *Auss was gründ vnnd vrsach Luthers dolmatschüng / vber das nawe testament / dem gemeinē man billich vorbotten worden sey.* A revised edition appeared the following year at Dresden, under the title, *Annotationes Hieronymi Emser vber Luthers naw Testamēt gebessert vnd emēdirt.*

[14] The first edition (Dresden: Stöckel, 1527) was entitled *Das naw testament nach lawt der Christlichē kirchen bewertē text / corrigirt / vñ widerumb zu recht gebracht.* The second edition (Leipzig: Schuman,

1528) was entitled *Das New Testamēt / So durch L. Emser sälige v̄teuscht / vnd' des Durch lewchtē Hochgebornē Furstē vn̄ herrē Herrē Georgē hertzogen zu Sachssen.* For reference to some other early editions, see note 10, above. Emser's death occurred on November 8, 1527, only a few months after the appearance of the first edition of his New Testament.

[15] See the comparisons presented by Kawerau, *op. cit.*, pp. 67-70; also those furnished by the present writer in his *Reformation Bibles in the Crossfire: The Story of Jerome Emser, His Anti-Lutheran Critique and His Catholic Bible Version* (Ann Arbor, Mich., 1961), pp. 101-110.

[16] *I.e.*, following the verse, as per the style used in the 1528 and 1529 Leipzig editions and in the Brethren's own Low-German translation. The first Emserian edition, as indicated in note 10, above, had its glosses in the page margins.

[17] This letter has been published in Friedrich Jenssen, *Emsers Neues Testament in niederdeutscher Übertragung* (Schwerin i. Mecklbg., 1933), pp. 6, 7.

[18] Concerning this trip, see, *e.g.*, Jenssen, *op. cit.*, pp. 7, 8; and Landeen, "The *Devotio Moderna* in Germany (Part IV)," *RSSCW*, XXII (1954), 67.

[19] The date 1530 appears on the title-page, but is probably that for the woodcut used there. See the discussion in Otto Leuze, "Ein doppelt denkwürdiges Neues Testament in der Bibelsammlung der Württembergischen Landesbibliothek in Stuttgart," in *Besondere Beilage des Staats-Anzeigers für Württemberg*, No. 2 (1926), 33.

[20] This document bears the date of June 28, 1532. It has been produced in full by Jenssen, *op. cit.*, pp. 8-10. The original is in the Rostock Stadt-Archiv.

[21] Jenssen, *op. cit.*, pp. 35-54, has furnished evidence that the Brethren used a Low-German Lutheran edition and the Lübeck version. The present writer would not be quite so hasty as Jenssen, however, in dismissing the Halberstadt Bible of 1522 and the Cologne Low-Saxon Bible of ca. 1480.

[22] See Landeen's comments on Arsenius in "The *Devotio Moderna* in Germany (Part IV)," *RSSCW*, XXII (1954), 70, 71.

[23] It is interesting to notice that the Brethren had earlier printed a work by the Reformation-minded Urbanus Rhegius, as well as a Danish edition of Luther's *Gebetbuch*. See Meltz, *op. cit.*, pp. 247, 244 (entries 55 and 30). The *Gebetbuch*, or *Bedebog* (as it was called in Danish), represented the translation of Poul Helgesen. But inasmuch as Helgesen was an opponent of "heresy" (he had written a *Reply to the Heretic Hans Michelsen of Malmö*), it is questionable that this work can be considered as good evidence of Protestant inclinations among the Rostock Brethren.

[24] In the gloss following Mt 4: 6 the Brethren use the term "kyndere de kettere" in place of Emser's "sohne / die ketzer." The meaning is, of course, substantially the same, and the gloss was certainly no improvement from the point of view of the Reformers.

Chapter 4

LUTHER'S DILEMMA:
RESTITUTION OR REFORMATION?

By LEONARD VERDUIN

(Reprinted in shortened form from *Dawn of Modern Civilization*, pp. 167-191)

"LUTHER's dilemma was that he wanted both a Confessional Church based on personal faith and a territorial Church including all in a given locality"—so it has been written recently.[1] It is with this dilemma that we shall be engaged here. We shall sketch in some detail its nature; then we shall note Luther's reduction of it.

Luther's dilemma resulted from two mutually exclusive delineations of the Christian Church. On his one hand was the view that the Church of Christ consists of changed men and women, persons who have been "converted"; that is, who have undergone a right-about-face in the core of their being. On his other hand was the view that the Church of Christ embraces all men, as they are, in a given political area. The former delineation of the Church operates with the concept of *Corpus Christi*, all true believers being members of this Body of Christ; the latter delineation of the Church operates with the concept of *Corpus Christianum*, the body of "christened" men and women who constitute "Christian" society. In the former ideology the Christian man stands in a situation of compositism, having men of radically different commitment all around him; in the latter ideology the Christian man stands in a society that is homogeneous, all members of that society being considered as having one and the same religious conviction. In the former system the Church consists of men who have joined together voluntarily; in the latter system men are in the Church by the happenstance

75

of being born in a "Christian" State. These were the alternatives Luther faced.

How did Luther come to be in this predicament? Whence the two delineations of the Church which lay at the root of his dilemma?

We submit that it was Luther's rediscovery of the New Testament (and therefore of the Church as delineated in that New Testament) which made the idea of a "Church based on personal faith" a genuine alternative for him. And we submit that it was Luther's respect for history, his conservative attitude toward what the Dutch call *het historisch gewordene* (that which has come about with the passing of time) that made the idea of the territorial Church a live option with him. The concept of the Church as laid down in the New Testament and the concept of the Church as laid down in historic tradition are two different things. Luther had a devoutly conservative attitude toward both the New Testament and *het historisch gewordene*—small wonder that he found himself torn betwixt the two.

The New Testament doctrine of the gathered Church, based as it is on the concept of grace that is sovereign and therefore selective, is one of Christianity's most radical ideas. Among other things, it introduces a new concept of society, the concept of societal compositism. To this innovation of New Testament Christianity we owe the idea of society-with-option; and this idea, the idea of society with option built into it, lies at the root of our freedoms.

To grasp the novelty of this pilot idea of authentic Christianity, let it be observed that pre-Christian society is sacral; that is, having a given religious loyalty to hold it together. Pre-Christian society is therefore optionless society. In pre-Christian society a man's religion is determined beforehand—every Navaho Indian (prior to the coming of the missionary, of course) is also an adherent of the Navaho religion; he has no option in the matter. And so it was regularly in pre-Christian society.

What Diana was for the Ephesians,[2] that some other deity, or college of deities, was for pre-Christian society in general. The Roman Empire had its college of deities, its god-pool, into which it solemnly ushered the object-of-worship of every tribe it conquered.[3] If the early Christians had been able and willing to have their Object-of-worship added to Rome's god-pool, all would have been smooth and easy. But the Christians' God was the God of *some;* and it was this that precipitated the persecutions and drove the Christians into the catacombs.

In a frantic attempt to eliminate the sacralism-wrecking new Faith, the emperors took some drastic steps, calculated to locate, and then annihilate, every adherent of the innovation. In the days of Decius every householder was ordered to procure an affidavit attesting loyalty to the ancestral sacralist order. There was a form to be filled in, reading as follows: "I, N.N., have always sacrificed to the gods and now in your presence I have, in keeping with the directive, sacrificed and caused a libation to be poured out, have tasted of the sacrificial victim; and I request that you, a public servant, certify the same." When subsequently a house-to-house check-up was conducted, the inability to produce the necessary billet was *prima facie* proof of addiction to the new Faith. If the suspect was unable to clear himself, he was thereupon condemned to capital punishment.[4]

In the midst of such Draconian procedures, men within the Church began to toy with the possibility of a new sacralism— a sacralism in which the Christian religion would occupy the place hitherto held by the ancestral faith of Rome. The introduction of such an order would automatically terminate the hardships that had hitherto been the lot of Christ's followers. It is to be understood that this looked good to many; Christian men were "sick and tired" of the persecutions.

But there was also opposition to this proposition. Men like Tertullian seem to have sensed the radicalness of such a change. The words sometimes attributed to him, *quid est imperatori cum ecclesia?* (What does the emperor have to do with the Church?), are the words of a man frightened at the prospect of Christianity forced into the sacralist frame. "It is a fundamental right, a privilege of nature, that every man should worship according to his own conviction. One man's religion neither harms nor helps another man. . . . It is not in the nature of religion to coerce to religion, which must be adopted voluntarily and not as a result of force"[5]—these words by Tertullian reveal a man agonizing over the very issues that were to precipitate the dilemma in which Luther found himself a dozen centuries later.

But "Christian sacralism" came.[6] With the conversion of Constantine (to be known all through medieval times as "the Great" because of the supposedly great good achieved in his time) the Christian faith was moved into the suite of rooms left empty by the removal of the erstwhile incumbent. Within the span of a single generation the roles were changed completely; now the Christian faith enjoyed all the privileges hitherto granted the ancestral faith; and the erstwhile hardship devolved now upon him who continued in the old ways. Those who lingered at the older shrines were made the victims of the same charges (in the identical words at times) to which the Christians had been exposed in the days of the earlier sacralism. By the end of the fourth century the simplest offerings set before the ancestral ethnic deities, even in household shrines, made the devotees subject to capital punishment. Attendance at religious gatherings in the signature of the now-outlawed paganism was punishable by death; indoctrination in the old religion was strictly forbidden, even if conducted in the privacy of the home; not-yet-baptized persons were required to attend classes leading to baptism. The death sentence awaited all who refused such baptism or who after having had it relapsed into the old ways.[7]

As all this was taking place, a man of vision, Hilary of Poitiers, lamented, "The Church now terrifieth with threats of exile and dungeon; and she who of old gained adherents to the faith in spite of exile and imprisonment now brings men to belief by compulsion. . . . She who was propagated by hunted priests now hunts priests in her turn. . . . This must be said in comparison with that Church that was handed down to us but which now we have lost; the fact is in men's eyes and cries aloud."[8] Here is the voice of a man in distress at the sight of the new sacralism. He is standing before alternatives, a "territorial Church including all in a given locality" contrasted with the Church "based on personal faith" which, as Hilary said, "now we have lost." Hilary was thus troubled by the same two alternatives which distressed Luther a dozen centuries later.

All through those twelve centuries the two delineations of the Church had stood in tension with each other. Beginning with the Donatist rebellion (which at heart protested against the Constantinian formula—against the new sacralism), and all through medieval times, the idea and the ideal of a Church of converted men was kept alive in the camp of the "heretics."[9] The Donatists insisted that *"agrum Dei in sola Africa reman-sisse"*;[10] and in the camp of the medieval dissenters this idea of a pure Church lived on.

The idea of a Church of true believers versus the idea of an everybody-embracing Church was a live option in the early years of Luther's career. And it was this option that precipitated Luther's dilemma. He had imbibed enough of the ideas of the pre-Reformation rebellion against "Christian sacralism" to make him kindly disposed toward the vision of the "heretics" and toward their delineation of the Church of Christ.

However, Luther was bound to discover that a frightfully high price would have to be paid for challenging consistently the ancestral order of "Christian sacralism." Zwingli had at one time reminded Luther of the fact that "not a few have there been in earlier times who knew the sum and substance of religion quite as well as you know it; but out of all Israel no one dared to take the risk of stepping forward to do battle, for all feared yon mighty Goliath as in the frightful weight of his armor he stood there in menacing stance."[11] Luther was soon to learn that "yon mighty Goliath" was still very formidable—for this "mighty Goliath" was the order of medieval sacralism, armed to the teeth to keep "Christendom" intact. Moreover, this "mighty Goliath" already had his eye on the intrepid young monk and was already hurling his usual barrage of taunts and big talk against any and all who, convinced that the Church of "Christendom" was a fallen creature, considered Restitution of the gathered Church a must. That there had been such Restitutionists around was well known to Luther.[12]

The age-old quarrel between the men of sacralist *Corpus Christianum* and the men of Restitutionist *Corpus Christi* was a quarrel with many ramifications. These two divergent views involve at once a score of elements of the Christian faith. We have space to enlarge upon only one of these—that dealing with *conduct.*

The Church of the New Testament is a Church of men and women of changed life. Its members are folk who have been "raised with Christ" and who therefore "seek the things that are above."[13] They "walk worthy of the calling"[14] and "bring forth fruits bespeaking repentance."[15] They are people who have undergone a moral "house-cleaning."

This feature of the gathered Church could not, however, survive the Constantinian innovation. The change to "Christian sacralism" had to bring with it a lowering of conductual requirement, a drift toward conductual averagism. In the new regime *Christian* conduct and *human* conduct became indifferentiable. If the Church was to embrace the total society, then it had to make room in its ranks for the behavior patterns of the rank and file. As Professor Frend has said, in his definitive work on the Donatist Church, "Once the premise of the Church as a body of the Elect has been dropped, then most of the puritanical beliefs with which this concept was associated, become obsolete."[16] The "puritanical beliefs" of primitive Christianity were indeed obsolete in medieval *Corpus Christianum.*

And because the medieval "heretic" was ever a person who had nostalgia for the pre-Constantinian order of things he was always a stickler for "conduct becoming the saints," always a man who harped on the behavioral requirements of New Testament Christianity. This was true of the Donatists; and it was true of all who took up the Restitutionist challenge after them. This feature of medieval "heresy," although by no means the only feature, was so prominent that it provided the German-speaking people with their most common word for the "heretic." The High-German *Ketzer* and the Low-German *ketter* are equivalent to the Greek word KATHAR pronounced with Teutonic vocal apparatus, and KATHAR is the stem of a Greek verb meaning *to cleanse*. A *Ketzer* is, then, a person who thinks in terms of a moral renovation.

Luther was plainly envious of the way of life that character-ized the "heretics." He praised the Waldensians of his time that "by God's grace there is found with you such a fine and disciplined way of life, no such gourmandizing and drinking, no such swearing and cursing, no such ostentation and wicked-ness, as is found with us. . . . We do not see how we could introduce such a fine and disciplined way of life, we who live in the middle of Sodom—God help us to something better!" Then, as if to soothe his conscience in the matter, Luther added, "But we do, however, have the right and the pure doctrine."[17] As we shall see, Luther's suggestion that *Rechtsinnigkeit* was an adequate substitute for *Rechtschaffenheit* was to bounce back on him and alienate from him those of his followers who had been conditioned by medieval Restitutionism.

Luther envied also the devout conduct of the Waldensians of Bohemia—whom he called *Pickards* or *Waldenses* interchange-ably. He was so enamored of their Christian behavior that he wrote of them, "Although they are by the papists vehemently condemned and dubbed as heretics, yet there is among them such a fine exterior and earnest zeal of discipline and good deportment as is not to be seen or heard among our own clergy and clerics; this is the fact, as our clergy will have to admit."[18]

But to lay down behavioral requirements for membership was to call into being "a Confessional Church based on personal faith"; and that implied the scuttling of the whole ancestral order with its "territorial Church including all in a given locality."

Luther was quite aware of the New Testament delineation

of the Church as a body of true believers; and he found it impossible to shrug off the idea of a gathered Church consisting of converted folk. In his *Deutsche Messe* (1526) Luther drew the plans for such a Church. He wrote, "Those who desire seriously to be Christians and confess the Gospel by word and by deed, these should enter their names in a ledger and meet somewhere in a house by themselves for the purpose of prayer, reading of Scripture, baptism, receiving the Sacrament and performing other Christian liturgical acts. . . ." But he was quite aware that to bring the Church back to the New Testament format was a big undertaking. For he added: "But I cannot gather such a Church or congregation as yet, for I do not have the people for it." He seems to have had something of conscience in the matter—an unwelcome conviction that he was dragging his feet—, for again he added, in self-defence it would seem: "If, however, the time comes that I must do it, so that I cannot with a good conscience refrain from it, I am ready to do my part." And then he gave evidence that he was quite aware of how radical it was to propose a believers' Church in the climate of sacralism. He indicated his fear to go ahead with the matter "lest it lead to faction, . . . for we Germans are a rough and noisy people, with whom it is not easy to start something new."[19]

Three years earlier, in 1523, Luther had already been thinking of restoring the Church to its New Testament *mode d'existence*. In his letter written in October to his friend Nicholas Hausmann, he had confided that "the plan is in future times to admit no one to communion unless he has been heard and has responded satisfactorily in regard to the faith; the rest we shall exclude."[20] This was tantamount to terminating the everybody-including Church and launching a believers' Church in its place. Aware of the radicalness of this step, Luther spoke of the plan as *future;* it was too radical to undertake immediately.

Similarly in his Sermon on *Grunen Donnerstag* Luther mulled over the possibility of bringing into being a Church of true believers. He declared in this sermon that if one were to take the Sacrament seriously "you will discover how few are Christian and how few would then go to the Sacrament. But in this way one could bring about (a thing I would like very much) that all those who believe aright could be assembled by themselves somewhere. I would have done it long ago but it has not yet been possible, for we have not preached and agitated enough as yet; for Christ did it that way too, he preached to the multitudes, as did the apostles after him, so that all could hear, believers and disbelievers alike. . . . That is the way we ought to do it. But we must not broadcast the Sacrament among the masses as the papacy does."[21] Here we have the blue-print for a "Church based on personal faith"; if executed, this plan would usher in the believers' Church. At the same time, however, Luther tried to perpetuate the public cult of sacralism with its "Church including all in a given territory." Needless to say, these plans were never executed; for a Church-of-believers cancels out a Church-of-the-masses.

Perhaps Luther revealed himself most clearly as a man impaled upon the horns of a dilemma in a conference with Caspar Schwenkfeld. The latter had come to confer with Luther and to "feel him out" as to his sentiments concerning the Restitutionist program. Schwenkfeld reported on this conference, saying: "Of the Church of the future I talked at length with him; how that this was the only possibility for separating the true Christians from the make-believe; how that otherwise there was no hope. He was also aware that church discipline must always accompany the Gospel; and that if discipline were not initiated there would be no improvement possible, but only progressive worsening—for it is apparent everywhere how it goes, everyone wants to pass for a Christian and boast himself of the name of Christ. Thereupon he replied that it grieved him greatly that no one was changing his deportment. . . . Of the Church of the future he said he had not as yet had any experience; although he intended to make a list of those who were Christian and intended to have their conduct scrutinized; and he was planning to preach to these in the cloister, a chaplain preaching to the rest in the *Pfarr"* (the main auditorium).[22] Here we see our Reformer keenly aware of the rightness of his visitor's ideal of the believers' Church; but he is not prepared to sever his ties with the past, not ready to drop the sacralist premise of a church that embraces the entire population. This was Luther's dilemma.

But Luther could not ride the fence in perpetuity. He would have to dissolve his dilemma. For he who takes the idea of the gathered Church seriously will have to declare war on the concept of the territorial Church; and he who embraces the idea of the territorial Church must become the enemy of the Restitutionist. And Luther did cast the die. We have seen him straddling the fence in regard to the gathering of true believers in the cloister versus the gathering of the masses in the *Pfarr*. He got off on the *Pfarr* side.

It seems that the events that lay around the kidnapping scene settled the matter for him. He realized that had it not been for the benefactions of Frederick, he would not have come out of the forest alive.[23] He gratefully accepted the hand of the secular power that was raised in his defence. But by accepting it Luther was drawn into the orbit of sacralism, was pulled in the direction of neo-Constantinianism. From this moment of decision it could be foreseen that the outcome of Luther's reformatory enterprise would be a *Landeskirche* rather than a Church of believers.

The decision cost Luther dearly. By his swing to the right he drove away those among his followers who had been influenced by the pre-Reformation Restitutionist tradition. These felt drawn to the other alternative, with which Luther was now breaking. In a word, when Luther got off on the *Pfarr* side, an element in his camp got off on the near side. These came to be known as "the Anabaptists." Thus "Anabaptists" was the name given to those in the left wing who abandoned Luther when he cast the die for the regional Church. This makes Anabaptism the post-Reformation camp of those who wanted "a Church based on personal faith,"—a group becoming articulate as soon as it became apparent that Luther was choosing for "a territorial Church including all in a given locality."

This interpretation of things we owe to Luther himself. He tells us that at the outset there were many in his parade who had earlier belonged to the dissent against the medieval order but who had maintained relative quiet because of the might of that order. He also tells us that these did not remain in his following but drew away from him to form the camp of the *Wiedertäufer*. He wrote: "In our times the doctrine of the Gospel, cleansed and restored, has gained and drawn to it many who had been in previous times suppressed by the tyranny of the Antichrist, the pope; however, there have forthwith gone from us Anabaptists, Sacramentarians, and other factionists . . . for they were not of us even though for a time they walked with us."[24] This tells the story. In the light of Luther's own report of what had happened, it becomes apparent that the crystallization of the Reformation in territorial churches or in parishes led by the political authorities gave the impulse for the building up of the Anabaptist circles.[25] C. A. Cornelius, one of the first to study Anabaptism from the sources rather than from the caricatures drawn by its enemies, already perceived the true situation when he wrote: "To Luther came others, people who prior to Luther had already distanced themselves from the church's doctrine and who were led by his activity to reveal their own ideas and to develop them into a system."[26] The words of John H. Yoder are also certainly to the point: "The study of Reformation history has in the past taken too little account of the deep changes which took place in the Reformers' thought and work. . . ."[27]

A great change did indeed take place when Luther made an end to his dilemma by casting his lot for neo-sacralism. The step cost him the support of the Restitutionists, and they became his enemies. The extreme hostility displayed by Luther and the other Reformers toward the Wiedertäufer reveals a well-known psychological pattern: the latter were the former's bad conscience. Had not the Anabaptists gone ahead, in the face of frightful odds, to do the very thing the Reformers had for practical reasons abandoned? After Luther's swing to the right, the very ambition he himself had entertained—to assemble a congregation of true believers—became highly objectionable. According to their earliest statements the Anabaptists' ambition was "to gather together those who are willing to accept Christ and obey the Word and follow in Christ's footsteps";[28] this is an ambition that lies very close to the one Luther cherished before he resolved his dilemma. The main point of difference is that whereas Luther drew back, the Anabaptists went ahead, come what may.[29]

The Anabaptists were not slow to detect the inconsistency between the Luther who had at one time expressed a fond desire to organize a believers' Church and the Luther who was now embarking upon a campaign against the Anabaptists for doing that very thing. They rubbed in his face the words he had put down in his *Deutsche Messe*. Speaking of their congregation of believers, they twitted their Lutheran antagonists. "Your own prophet Martin Luther," they declared, "has written about such gatherings, in a little book entitled *Deutsche Messe*, as follows: 'Men ought to gather in a place apart behind closed doors.' . . . but he added, 'I am not brave enough to make a beginning with that sort of thing, lest it be considered an act of sedition.' "[30] These were bitter words, bitter in their pointedness; and they made Luther bitter toward the "Wiedertäufer, Sacramentschwärmer und andere Rottengeister" who had abandoned his cause.

The honeymoon between Luther and the Restitutionists was over. The latter began to pick out the flaws in Luther's program, and he was quick to respond in kind. Among men of Restitutionist sympathies it began to be said that Luther was welding the Cross of Christ to the sword of the emperor, to the forces of darkness themselves.[31] The integration of Luther's Reform with the secular power was in the eyes of the men of the gathered Church a major calamity, a matter that spoiled everything that otherwise was good in Luther's work. To quote: "These two, Luther and Zwingli, have exposed all the tricks and the knavery of the papal holiness as they sought as with thunderclaps to knock the bottom out of it; they have not, however, raised up a better. But rather, the moment they integrated themselves with the secular power . . . it went with them as with the man who in mending an old kettle only makes the hole bigger. And they have raised up a people altogether callous in sin."[32]

As the last quotation makes apparent, the matter of conduct (certain to come up whenever sacralism is discussed) played an important part in the tensions that were now developing between the Luther who had dissolved his dilemma in favor of the territorial Church and the people who had chosen the other alternative. With Luther's return to sacralism his movement was doomed to a return to conductual averagism. Those who had left his camp began to look for the tell-tale marks of sacralism—not least in the area of conduct. And they found plenty to censure. Moreover, Luther's assault upon the Epistle of James supplied the Restitutionist critics with a good point of departure. His treatment of James—always a favorite book with men of Restitutionist sympathies—left his flank open to attack; and the Anabaptists were quick to find this vulnerable spot. Soon the two factions were in irreconcilable conflict touching conduct patterns.

The Anabaptists were from the outset crusaders for Christian conduct. As early as 1524 Conrad Grebel had written, "Ietzunt wil iederman in glichsendem glouben selig werden, on frucht des gloubens . . . on rechte Christenliche brüch."[33] Now the Restitutionists began to assail the very *sola fide* emphasis of Luther. Conditioned as they were by the Restitutionists' long battle against the conductual averagism of the medieval church they found the *sola fide* of Luther hard to accept—or even understand.[34] From the outset the Anabaptists missed in the Reformers that call to "conduct becoming the saints" on which Restitutionism had thrived. They said that the Reformers "throw works without faith so far to one side that they erect a faith without works."[35] And this criticism on the part of the Anabaptists became more and more emphatic as the years went by. Some of Menno Simons' most eloquent passages are those in which he takes the Reformers to task for their conductual averagism.[36]

What was taking place, theologically speaking, is that Luther's one-sided emphasis upon the forensic aspect of God's redemptive enterprise, his heavy emphasis upon justification by faith, was colliding with an equally one-sided emphasis on the moral aspect of the redemptive enterprise. The two, again theologically speaking, are meant to complement each other, not cancel each other out. Luther's theology was a theology of what God has done *for* men; the Restitutionists had a theology of what He does *in* men. Luther's system was built around the concept of justification—a forensic concept; the Restitutionists, early and late, adhered to a system controlled by the concept of sanctification—a moral concept. From a theological point of view, the tension between these two camps was unnecessary and highly deplorable, for they represent complementary thrusts in authentic Christian theology.[37]

Whether it was Luther's one-sided emphasis upon the forensic or the Restitutionists' equally one-sided emphasis on the moral need not detain us here, but the fact is that the tension led to complete estrangement between Luther and the "Pickarts," as he called the Bohemian Brethren. These had sent some of their young men to Wittenberg to prepare for the ministry. But (from the Brethren's point of view) their stay in Wittenberg spoiled them completely; upon their return they actually attacked the traditional puritanism of the Brethren, calling it a denial of Christian liberty. Needless to say, the Brethren sent no more of their sons. Years later, this unhappy experience with Wittenberg still rankled in the bosom of the Brethren. They began to look to the more westerly areas of the Reformation for the friendship they needed so badly, sending one Czerwenka to Strassburg, to confer with the leaders of the Reform in those parts. Czerwenka there spoke quite freely of the Brethren's disillusionment in regard to Luther's movement.[38] Luther, no doubt smarting under the experience, now began to refer to his erstwhile friends, whom he had admired so ardently, as "geistliche Juden und elenden Ketzer. . . . O ihr gotteslästerer und Christi Verräther"! The reason? Because they "von den bösen Christen fliehen und zu ihnen selbst im Winckel kriechen."[39]

The sources testify voluminously to the fact that the defection of the Anabaptists from the camp of the Reformers was in a large way due to the return to the idea of "a territorial Church including all in a given locality." As one Anabaptist spokesman put it, in 1538:

> While still in the national church we obtained much instruction from the writings of Luther, Zwingli, and others. . . . Yet we found a great lack as regards repentance, conversion, and the true Christian life. Upon these my mind was set. I waited and hoped for a year or two . . . but no beginning was made toward true Christian living. . . . True repentance and Christian love were not in evidence. . . . Then God sent His messengers, Conrad Grebel and others . . . who had surrendered themselves in the doctrine of Christ. . . . With their assistance a congregation was formed in which repentance was in evidence by newness of life in Christ.[40]

Luther's return to the territorial Church had made impossible the recovery of Christian conductual requirements—and so the only thing left for people of Restitutionist sympathies was to leave the ranks of the Reformers and organize separately.

Soon the devout deportment of the seceders became their strong talking point. At times Luther, now on the defensive, tried to justify himself; at times he tried a centuries-old escape (used all through medieval times) to the effect that the excellent conduct of the "heretics" was nothing but a trick of the devil, bait put on the hook so as to catch more fish! In this mood of self-justification he said in the year 1533: "Doctrine and life are to be distinguished from each other. With us conduct is as bad as with the papists; we do not oppose and condemn them on account of conduct. Hus and Wyclif, who made an issue of conduct, were not aware of this. . . . Still others have assailed the evil life; but to treat of doctrine—that is to take hold where the hair is short."[41] In the meantime, observers were saying

of the camp of the Lutherans that the idea of evangelical freedom was carried so far that "anyone who speaks of God and
of the Christian way of life, or who is concerned about his own
moral improvement passes with them for an arch-Anabaptist."[42]

The rift between Luther and those who had chosen the other
horn of his dilemma was now beyond repair. The Anabaptists
continued, with considerable success, their original objective of
gathering together a church of converted people; and in Luther's
bosom must have rankled the thought that he himself had at
one time said it could not be done. At any rate, he left no
chance unutilized to chide the Anabaptists for having seceded
because of the conductual averagism that prevailed in Lutheran
territorial churches. In a sermon on the Parable of the Tares
he wrote:

> This Parable is a comfort over against the *Schwärm-
> geister* and all who take offence at the imperfections of
> the church. For from the beginning of Christendom,
> heretics have maintained that the church of Christ must
> be holy and without sin. Because they saw that some
> in it were the servants of sin, therefore they denied
> forthwith that the Church was the Church; and they
> organized sects which they then liked to consider the
> Church. This is the origin of the Donatists and the
> Cathars and many others, also of the Anabaptists in
> our days. All these cry out in chorus that the Church
> is not the Church, because they see sinners and god-
> less people mixed in; and they have separated from her.
> It is the part of wisdom not to be offended if evil men
> and heretics come and go in the Church. . . . The
> greatest comfort of all is to know that they do no harm
> but that we must allow the tares to be mixed in. . . .
> The *Schwärmer*, who do not allow tares among them,
> actually bring about that there is no wheat with them.
> By their passion for wheat only and a pure Church
> they bring about that they are not even a Church but
> just a sect of the devil.[43]

In connection with "wolves in sheep's clothing" (Matthew
7:15) Luther declared:

You may see this fulfilled in the Anabaptists; there you do not hear so much as one little swear word; their dress, food, drink, is simple and plain; they spend much time with the Word of God; they pray a great deal, are patient in suffering and not given to vengeance. Now all this is in itself not bad, and one could wish that in these matters all men were like them. But for this reason to consider their teachings acceptable and to follow them, of that Christ says, "Beware of them." Such a harmful and shameless wolf hides under their fine sleek hide in that the Anabaptists make so excellent a showing in their outward lives.[44]

On still another occasion Luther said of the Anabaptists:

When they look at us and see the offensive defects with which Satan distorts our churches, then they deny that we are the Church and say that they are unable to lift themselves over this obstacle. In like manner the Donatists were minded. . . . Men ought not to dispute about the Church that way. . . . Whatever remains of sin, this verily offends these spiritual Donatists . . . but it does not offend God, seeing that for the sake of faith in Christ he excuses it and forgives.[45]

At this time Urbanus Rhegius, Luther's colleague, wrote a polemic against the Anabaptists, at Luther's suggestion and under Luther's coaching. The occasion was something which the Anabaptist Bernhard Knipperdollinck had written, to the effect that in the churches headed by the Reformers there was "nothing but publicans, drunkards, gluttons and fornicators." To this Rhegius replied:

Here Bernhard resorts to a typically Donatist trick. They condemned and abandoned Christendom because of the false and wicked Christians, as though they were themselves altogether holy and angelic. . . . Nevertheless, there have always been some right-minded and devout Christians in the mass—we hope they are to be found among us also. And the fact that there are wicked scoundrels under the cloak of the Gospel is none of our business; we did not instruct them to drink and gourmandize, to be immoral or avaricious. . . .

However, we are not minded on account of some evil
fish to rend the net, as the Anabaptist Bernhard is
doing at Münster. He gives himself away at this point
and reveals his Anabaptist heart and shows that he has
the very same Anabaptist devil in him that blinded
the Donatists in Africa. They opened their eyes in Africa
and saw with hypocritical eyes that many wicked folk
were adorning themselves with the Christian name,
men who were at heart downright pagan. And so they
separated themselves from Christendom and pretended
to raise up a truly reformed Church, one in which there
were none but living saints; and they became so holy
in their way of thinking that they considered as bogus
and void the baptism which had been administered
by wicked priests or ministers. And they baptized anew,
thinking thereby to raise up true holiness. They also
chided St. Augustine vigorously, as though he too was
of the assembly of the wicked who were betrayers and
scoundrels. Thereupon Augustine replied that there
were indeed wicked people in his Church but that the
efficacy of the Sacrament did not depend on the
sanctity of the dispenser. . . . Moreover, the external
association of good and evil poses no threat to the
salvation of the good, seeing that they do not assent
to the evil and the wickedness. . . . We are not to make
a division; he who nevertheless separates himself from
the Church becomes a schismatic and a heretic. Let
Bernhard consider himself told off; for he is a new Donatist, who has taken offence at the lives of evil men,
and he has sought at Münster to organize a spotlessly
holy church, one in which there are only saints, a net
without any foul fish—he and his company, separated
from Christendom. . . . I would verily rather be a
coarse publican or a patent sinner in the Christian
Church than the holiest Pharisee of all in the heretics'
cave of Bishop Bernhard.[46]

There can be no doubt that if placed before the alternatives
here posited, the Anabaptists would have elected and defended
the other alternative with just as much abandon.

It goes without saying that Luther's choice between the two

alternatives posed in his dilemma was momentous. It determined the pattern of life in Germany for centuries to come, as well as in other lands where Lutheranism took deep root. Luther's solution was a solution touching the relationship of Church and State, as any solution of this problem is bound to be.

Whether Luther's choice was good or bad will be argued even now. But the words of Walter Hobhouse must give pause to all who ponder the matter and to all who as historians deal with the Reformation and with its Luther:

> Long ago I came to believe that the great change in relations between the Church and the World which began with the Conversion of Constantine is not only a decisive turning-point in the history but is also the key to many of the practical difficulties of the present day, and that the Church of the future is destined more and more to return to a condition of things somewhat like that which prevailed in the Ante-nicene Church; that is to say, that instead of pretending to be coextensive with the world it will confess itself the Church of a minority, will accept a position involving a more conscious antagonism with the World, and will, in return, gain in some measure its former coherence.[47]

NOTES

1. Roland H. Bainton, *Here I Stand: A Life of Martin Luther* (New York & Nashville, Tenn.: Abingdon Press, 1950), p. 311.

2. Cf. Acts 19:23ff.

3. For a description of the procedure, cf. Minucius Felix' *Octavius,* VI.

4. The General Library of the University of Michigan has, among its papyri, an executed copy of this formulary.

5. Miner Searle Bates, *Religious Liberty: An Inquiry* (New York: Harper and Brothers, 1945), p. 137 quoting.

6. We enclose the expression in quotation marks because we think the combination of this noun and this adjective to be anomalous.

7. Cf. Leo Pfeffer, *Church, State, and Freedom* (Boston: Beacon Press, 1953), p. 13.

8. George Gordon Coulton, *Inquisition and Liberty* (London and Toronto: Heinemann, 1938), p. 16.

9. The very word is revealing: Derived from the Greek verb *hairein,*

meaning "to exercise option," it denotes the man who assumes that in the matter of religious loyalty there is a choice.

10. This expression is ascribed to the Donatists by Augustine. See his *Contra Epistolam Parmeniani*, II, 2:5.

11. The expression occurs in Zwingli's *Freundliche Auslegung*.

12. "In den zwölf Jahrhunderten, welche zwischen dem 3 und 14 Jahrhundert liegen, haben Versuche niemals gefehlt, die Bande der Priesterkirche und der Staatskirche zu sprengen und die 'apostolische Gemeindeverfassung' wiederherzustellen."—Adolph Harnack, "Die Didache und die Waldenser," in *Texte und Untersuchungen zur Geschichte der Altchristlichen Literatur* (Leipzig: Hinrichs'sche Buchhandlung, 1886), Band II, p. 269.

13. Cf. Col. 3:1.

14. Cf. Eph. 4:1.

15. Cf. Acts 3:8.

16. W. H. C. Frend, *The Donatist Church* (Oxford: Clarendon Press, 1952), p. 322.

17. Cf. Luther's *Werke*, St. Louis ed., Vol. XIX, kol. 1337.

18. In the Preface prefixed by Luther to the Catechism of the Bohemian Brethren, which he saw through the presses.

19. Cf. Luther's *Werke*, Weimar ed., Vol. XIX, p. 75.

20. Cf. Luther's *Werke*, Weimar ed., *Briefwechsel*, Band III, p. 183.

21. Cf. Luther's *Werke*, Weimar ed., Vol. XII, p. 485. Earlier in the same *Sermon* Luther had said that to extend the Sacrament to unbelieving men was "nicht vil anders . . . denn wenn du es einer Sau in hals stössest; ein spot ist es, unnd ein unere des Sacraments."

22. Cf. Schwenkfeld's letter to Friedrich von Walden, *Epistolar*, 1570, III, p. 43.

23. Cartoons were already in circulation depicting Luther as "the German Goose," ready to be served on a platter—the point being that Luther was going the way of John Hus, to the fire ("hus" is Bohemian for "goose").

24. Cf. Luther's *Werke*, St. Louis ed., Vol. II, kol. 1417 (commentary on Genesis 41:45).

25. It was this very issue that had aligned the Donatists against the Catholics. As Martroye has said of these two camps, "On ne commença à se détester reciproquement que le jour où le pouvoir impérial intervint dans la discussion religieuse. La haine fut la conséquence des rigeurs ordonées contra les donatistes, quand l'intérêt de la paix publique força les empereurs de revenir à la vieille doctrine romaine de la religion subordonnée au prince." Cf. Vol. 76 of *Revue des Questions Historiques* (1904), p. 365.

26. C. A. Cornelius, *Geschichte des Münsterischen Aufruhrs* (Leipzig, 1855), Book II, p. 7.

27. John H. Yoder, "The Prophetic Dissent," in *The Recovery of the Anabaptist Vision* (Scottdale: Herald Press, 1957), p. 104.

28. According to Zwingli's testimony (Cf. *Corpus Reformatorum*, Vol. 91, p. 169), "Sige Simon von Höng zu im und meister Löwenn kommen und habe sy beid angefochtenn, das sy ein besonnder volck und kilchenn söttind uffrichtenn und ein christenlich volck darin han, das da zum aller unschuldigisten lepte und ouch dem euangelio bickleib und anhengig weri. . . . Da habind sy inn all weg güttlich und früntlich abgewyssenn. . . ." Apparently Luther's dilemma was Zwingli's dilemma also; and Luther's solution was also Zwingli's.

29. We who live where separation of Church and State is axiomatic have difficulty in realizing how radical, revolutionary, almost nihilistic, the Anabaptist platform seemed to be to contemporaries. To them it appeared to be the beginning of the end.

30. G. L. Schmidt, *Justus Menius* (Gotha, 1867), I, 141f.

31. This rather low view of the magistrate occurs frequently in the literature stemming from Restitutionist sources. The reason for such a view has been sought in various directions. It seems best to link it to the fact that as the Restitutionists experienced the magistrate he was an agent in the employ of the fallen everybody-embracing Church; and since in this vision the everybody-embracing Church is Antichrist, it follows that his agents (*in casu,* the magistrate) cannot be much good.

32. A. J. F. Zieglschmidt, *Die Aelteste Chronik der Hutterischen Brüder* (Ithaca, New York: Cayuga Press, 1943), p. 42. A passage, very similar and yet not identical, from the hand of an unnamed Anabaptist, is quoted in Christiaan Sepp, *Kerkhistorische Studiën* (Leiden: E. J. Brill, 1885), p. 4.

33. Quoted, *inter alia,* in Cornelius, *op. cit.,* Vol. II, Beilage I.

34. *Sola fide* was meant by Luther to mean "faith unassisted"; some in the Restitutionist camp seem to have understood the expression to mean "faith unassociated." Luther's advice, *"pecca fortiter,"* gave some ground for the Restitutionists' interpretation of *sola fide.* Luther's expression *"simul justus et peccator"* contributed to the confusion also.

35. "Verwerpen also die wercken sonder gheloove dat sy een gheloove sonder wercke oprichten." Cf. *Bibliotheca Reformatoria Neerlandica* (The Hague: Nijhoff, 1903-1914), Vol. V, p. 628.

36. Menno wrote, for example, of the Lutherans: "They strike up a Psalm, 'der Strick ist entzwei und wir sind frei!' while the beer and the wine verily run from their drunken mouths and noses. Anyone who can but recite this on his thumb, no matter how carnally he lives, is a good evangelical man and a precious brother." Cf. *The Complete Writings of Menno Simons* (Scottdale, Penn.: Herald Press, 1956), p. 334, in the present writer's translation.

37. The two thrusts have been nicely combined in the old hymn *Rock of Ages,* where we have: "Be of sin the double cure, save from wrath and make me pure!"

38. Czerwenka's not very complimentary report on Lutheranism may be read in the original Czech, accompanied by a rather free summary in German, in *Fontes Rerum Austriacarum,* Band XIX, Abth. II (1859), p. 64f.

39. Luther's *Werke,* St. Louis ed., Vol. V, kol. 901.

40. Cf. *Acta des Gespraechs zwueschenn predicantenn Uund Tauffbruederenn Ergangen, Inn der Statt Bernn. . . .* (Vol. 80 of certain *Unnützen Papiere* held in the Staatsarchiv des Kantons Bern). The Mennonite Historical Library at Goshen, Indiana, has a copy of this manuscript.

41. Luther's *Werke,* Weimar ed., Vol. I, p. 294.

42. Cf. Cornelius, *op. cit.,* Vol. II, p. 45.

43. Luther's *Werke,* St. Louis ed., Vol. VII, kol. 200.

44. Luther's *Werke,* St. Louis ed., Vol. XIIIa, kol. 799.

45. Luther's *Werke,* St. Louis ed., Vol. V, kol. 747.

46. Urbanus Rhegius, *Widderlegung der Münsterischen newen Valentianer und Donatisten erkanntnus* (Wittenberg, 1535). No pagination; passage quoted occurs near the end.

47. Walter Hobhouse, *The Church and the World in Idea and in History* (London: Macmillan, 1910), p. IX.

HISTORIOGRAPHY

Chapter 5

THE PEASANTS' WAR IN GERMANY: SOME OBSERVATIONS ON RECENT HISTORIOGRAPHY

By ROBERT N. CROSSLEY

THROUGHOUT the Middle Ages, the Renaissance period, and into early modern times, peasant unrest culminating in peasant uprisings was not uncommon in European history. Such revolts plagued practically all of the governing authorities in the European states. Until the 16th century, however, these uprisings were for the most part local and sporadic. The major cause for peasant unrest was usually economic. The revolt might start because of a poor harvest brought on by unfavorable weather conditions. Or the feudal lord might raise either the dues or the services from the peasants on his land. Whether the peasant was a free man or bound to the soil by serfdom, living was a precarious and dangerous matter. When that living was made more difficult by a member of the nobility, the peasant or group of peasants was bound to offer some resistance.

The Peasant Revolt in the German lands during the years 1524-1526 was one which dwarfed previous peasant uprisings. It seemed to many contemporaries that all Germany was in flames, that all the peasants were in revolt against the legally constituted authorities. And various historians writing on the subject have characterized the revolt as a war: hence the "Peasants' War" in Germany. This terminology itself distinguishes the events of 1524-26 from earlier revolts or uprisings. Some may disagree with the use of the word "war" to describe the revolt since there was no unity among the peasant forces militarily, politically, or economically, nor was there any overall command. Although there was very little cooperation between the peasant forces, there was, on the other hand, cooperation and consultation between many of the forces of the various princes. Such cooperation existed even after the conclusion of the war, particularly against those erring nobles who for one reason or another had thrown in their lot with the peasants.

It is impossible in this brief essay to discuss the entire historiography of the "Peasants' War." Even a cursory examination of Karl Schottenloher's *Bibliographie zur deutschen Geschichte im Zeitalter der Glaubensspaltung 1517-1585* will demonstrate the tremendous amount of work that has been done on this subject. A continuing examination of historical journals in the United States and in Europe also shows that the Peasants' War remains of current interest to many scholars. I would like, however, to focus attention on some of the major trends (particularly the more recent ones) in this historiography of that War and to illustrate these trends by reference to a few examples in each of several general categories: (1) histories and source collections relating to the War itself; (2) treatments of Thomas Münzer (what might be called the "Münzer Revival"); and (3) explorations of the relationship between Münzer and Anabaptism. Admittedly, various of the books that will be cited could and do fall into more than one category.

The first general category consists of three kinds of works: (1) general histories of the War; (2) regional histories of the War; and (3) collections of documents relating to the War. In each of these categories, the number of publications is large indeed. Among the general histories, the recent historiography of the War begins, of course, with the work of Wilhelm Zimmermann, *Allgemeine Geschichte des grossen Bauernkrieges* (3 vols.; Stuttgart, 1841-43). Although over a century old, this work cannot be neglected by anyone interested in the War nor by anyone interested in the historiography. Even though many of the more recent collections of documents were not available to Zimmermann, he performed a herculean task in his synthesis of the conflict. Friedrich Engels in the preface to his own work on the war pays tribute to Zimmermann and admits quite candidly that his work is based almost exclusively on Zimmermann's three volumes. Engels first published his own study in a series of articles in the *Neue Rheinische Zeitung* in 1850. It came out in book form in the 1870's and in English translation appears under the title *The Peasant War in Germany*. This study, which Engels was in the process of revising and expanding when he died, manifests the influence which the events of 1848-49 had on the writing of history during that period.

Except for English translations of Engels' work, the only general survey of the Peasants' War in the English language remains E. Belfort Bax, *The Peasants War in Germany 1525-1526* (London and New York, 1899). The best general history in any language remains Günther Franz, *Der deutsche Bauernkrieg* (2 vols.; München & Berlin, 1933-35; plus further editions including Darmstadt, 1956 & 1965 [the 1965 edition is called the "7th" edition]). Although Franz has been labeled by his colleagues in East Germany as a Fascist historian (see the register in the work by M. M. Smirin discussed below), no comparable work has yet been written. Nevertheless, other general studies should be mentioned: Otto H. Brandt, *Der deutsche Bauernkrieg* (Jena, 1929); Karl Hartfelder, *Zur Geschichte des Bauernkriegs in Südwestdeutschland* (Stuttgart, 1884); Hugo Hantsch, *Der deutsche Bauernkrieg* (Würzburg, 1925); Alexandre Weill, *Histoire de la grande guerre des paysans* (3rd ed.; Paris, 1860). All of these studies have been superseded by the work of Günther Franz. One special study of great value, however, is the work of Heinz Kamnitzer, *Zur Vorgeschichte des deutschen Bauernkrieges* (Berlin, 1953; c. 1952).

Regional studies are also quite numerous, as Schottenloher indicates. There are special studies for practically every region of Germany which was involved in the War. A brief sampling is sufficient to indicate the extent and scope of these studies: Hermann Barge, *Der süddeutsche Bauernkrieg in zeitgenössischen Quellenzeugnissen* (Leipzig, 1914); H. Zins, "Aspects of the Peasant Rising in East Prussia in 1525," *Slavonic and East European Review*, 38 (1959), pp. 178-187; Valentin Lötscher, *Der deutsche Bauernkrieg in der Darstellung und im Urteil der zeitgenössischen Schweizer* (Basel, 1943).

In the 1920's the Saxon Commission for History began the publication of documents relating to the Peasants' War in central or middle Germany, edited by Otto Merx, Günther Franz, and Walther Peter Fuchs, *Akten zur Geschichte des Bauernkriegs in Mitteldeutschland* (Leipzig, 1923, 1934, and Jena, 1942; also reprint edition of Aalen, 1964). When Franz revised his two-volume study of the War in 1956, he also began the preparation of a companion volume of documents and sources. This appeared under the title *Quellen zur Geschichte des Bauernkrieges* (München, 1963). An interesting review of this collection has been written by Hans J. Hillerbrand in the *Archiv für Reformationsgeschichte*, 56 (1965), pp. 259, 260.

It is still necessary for the student of the Peasants' War to be constantly on the lookout for articles in the journals dealing with new sources or dealing with the historiography of the War itself. Among such articles which have appeared fairly recently are Max Steinmetz' "Reformation und Bauernkrieg in der Historiographie der DDR," which was published in *Zeitschrift für Geschichtswissenschaft*, 8 (1960), Sonderheft, pp. 142-162; and Fritz Zimmermann's "Unbekannte Quellen zur Geschichte des Bauernkrieges 1525," which appeared in the *Zeitschrift für bayerische Landesgeschichte* in 1964.

Even though interpretation and lack of objectivity are present in the general studies, regional histories, and even in the selection of documents to be published (no one can deny that interpretation is present in the work by Engels), nevertheless it is in the second category of works relating to the War that a myriad of interpretations appears. This second category, as we have noted, may be termed the "Münzer Revival." Surprising as it may seem, Thomas Münzer remained relatively unknown as a Reformation figure until the 19th century. And it is only in the 20th century that Münzer has come to be considered one of the greatest of the reformers—according to some, even superior to Luther himself. In fact, the Reformation is sometimes divided into the People's or Volksreformation led by Münzer and the Princely or Herrenreformation led by Luther.

The new emphasis in the 20th century begins with the work of Ernst Bloch, *Thomas Münzer als Theologe der Revolution* (Berlin, 1921; reissued in 1960), also published in a French edition as *Thomas Münzer, Théologien de la révolution,* translated by Maurice de Gandillac (Paris, 1964). It should be noted, too, that those great Reformation scholars Heinrich Böhmer and Otto Brandt produced studies of Münzer in the 1920's and 1930's. However, it is really with M. M. Smirin, *Die Volksreformation des Thomas Münzer und der grosse Bauernkrieg,* translated from Russian by H. Nichtweiss (2nd ed.; Berlin, 1956), and Alfred Meusel, *Thomas Müntzer und seine Zeit. Mit einer Auswahl der Dokumente des grossen deutschen Bauernkrieges* (Berlin, 1952), that the revival accelerates. In these two works it is clearly the interpretation of the authors that Münzer led a popular reformation whereas Luther was a tool of the princes.

Meusel and Smirin have made it necessary for a more detailed study of Münzer to take place. Although Carl Hinrichs had previously begun to work on Münzer (*Müntzer, Thomas. Politische Schriften mit Kommentar* [Halle, 1950]), the real deluge of literature came after the works of Meusel and Smirin in 1952 and 1956. A sampling will be sufficient here: Georg Baring, "Hans Denck und Thomas Müntzer in Nürnberg 1524," *Archiv für Reformationsgeschichte,* 50 (1959), pp. 145-181; E. Gordon Rupp, "Thomas Müntzer, Hans Huth and the 'Gospel of all Creatures,'" *Bulletin of the John Rylands Library,* 43 (1961), pp. 492-519; Thomas Nipperdey, "Theologie und Revolution bei Thomas Müntzer," *Archiv für Reformationsgeschichte,* 54 (1963), pp. 145-181; George W. Forell, "Thomas Münzer: Symbol and Reality," *Dialog,* 2 (1963), pp. 12-23; Abraham Friesen, "Thomas Müntzer in Marxist Thought," *Church History,* 34 (1965), pp. 306-327; and E. Gordon Rupp, "Thomas Müntzer: Prophet of Radical Christianity," *Bulletin of the John Rylands Library,* 48 (1966), pp. 467-487. Thomas Münzer is also studied in a recent work by Hans J. Hillerbrand, *A Fellowship of Discontent* (New York, 1967).

The contest between those supporting Münzer and those supporting Luther is far from over. Meusel and Smirin have demonstrated the influence of contemporary 20th-century events and ideologies in their interpretation of the 16th century. More works of Münzer must be found. Letters, sermons, political writings, and works on the liturgy are all important for an understanding of the man and his role in the great events of the 1520's. Although many have already come to a judgment, reserve must still be exercised.

The Münzer revival has also led to the third category of writings on the Peasants' War, the category which concerns the relationship of Münzer to Anabaptism—or to put it another way, the relationship of Anabaptism to the terrible events of 1525. Was Münzer an Anabaptist? Was he the forerunner of the Anabaptism of the 16th century? Was Anabaptism a cause of the Peasant Uprising in 1525? In treating such questions, perhaps the greatest contribution has been made by the editors and contributors to the *Mennonite Quarterly Review*. Since its founding in the 1920's this journal has uniformly contained excellent articles on the history of 16th-century Anabaptism. Two of the more recent articles will suffice to illustrate the trend in this especially fine journal: Robert Friedmann, "Thomas Muentzer's Relation to Anabaptism," 31 (1957), pp. 75-87; and Eric W. Gritsch, "Thomas Muentzer and the Origins of Protestant Spiritualism," 37 (1963), pp. 172-194. One of the best books on this subject, but also broader in its treatment, is John Stanley Oyer, *Lutheran Reformers Against Anabaptists* (The Hague, 1964). This is one of the most valuable recent works on those early radicals who so disturbed Luther in that critical period from 1521 through 1525, including Karlstadt and the Zwickau Prophets Nicholas Storch and Marcus Stübner. Such radicals, who were called Schwärmer by Luther and his associates, have caused considerable difficulty for students of the early Reformation and especially for those interested in the origins of Anabaptism. Since the Zwickau Prophets were loosely associated with Münzer and later with the Peasants' War, it seems necessary either to classify them as Anabaptists or to disassociate them from that movement entirely.

The recent writers, such as those just mentioned, have for the most part attempted, and I think rather successfully, to distinguish between Thomas Münzer's religious views and activity and the Anabaptism of the late 1520's. The great movement called "16th-century Anabaptism" is generally considered to have begun no earlier than 1525-26. Hence those who caused the Peasants' War or who participated in it were not at that time Anabaptists. The fact that certain interpretations of Münzer and the Zwickau Prophets reveal a medieval origin indicates that even the broad movement of the Reformation was not responsible for their radical programs and peculiarities.

One further aspect of the historiography of the Peasants' War, in addition to the three mentioned above, deserves at least brief mention here: Luther's relationship to the Uprising, a question which has been given considerable attention in the literature. In an earlier essay* I have dealt with the more prominent criticisms of Luther's activities at the time, and I shall not repeat myself here. However, it may be observed that Luther opposed the peasants and their leaders partly out of ignorance of their aims and objectives and partly, too, because of fear and anger at distortions and misinterpretations of his teachings. John Stanley Oyer, in his excellent book already mentioned, has shown that much of Luther's information about the so-called radicals was either wrong or distorted. Much was second hand. Much, too, came from their enemies. Some even came from trial records. Most was designed to place these radicals in as bad a light as possible. Nevertheless, no one can deny that the teachings of Münzer and Karlstadt bore little resemblance to

---

Editor's Note: This essay appears as Chapter I of the present volume, pp. 31-44, above.

what Luther taught. So Luther opposed them because of what the radicals and their activities would do to the movement which he was leading.

On the question of Luther's relationship to the Peasants' War, I mention but a few of the more recent works which can be examined with profit: M. Greschat, "Luther's Haltung im Bauern-krieg," *Archiv für Reformationsgeschichte*, 56 (1965), pp. 31-47; Heinz F. Mackensen, "Historical Interpretation and Luther's Role in the Peasant Revolt," *Concordia Theological Monthly*, 35 (1964), pp. 197-209; Hayo Gerdes, *Luthers Streit mit den Schwärmern um das rechte Verstandnis des Gesetzes Mose* (Göttingen, 1955); and Karl Kupisch, *Feinde Luthers. Vier historische Bildnisse* (Berlin, 1951). Kupisch treats Münzer on pp. 67-94.

The Peasants' War in Germany and the historiography of that War in the 19th and 20th centuries demonstrate again the influence of contemporary events on the writing of history. Recent historiography also demonstrates the need for continued investigation and research. Although much has been done, much remains to be done. Münzer is probably the main key to the whole matter. His political ideas, his role as a church reformer, his place in the early Reformation—these must still be examined and assessed. Although the Peasants' War took place over 400 years ago, it continues to be a vital and valid topic for the student of history.

Chapter 6

LUTHER'S SCHOOLING IN MAGDEBURG:
A NOTE ON RECENT VIEWS

By Kenneth A. Strand

In a letter to Magdeburg Burgomaster Claus Storm in 1522, Martin Luther mentions the time when he (Luther) and a companion named Hans Reinecke went to school "to the Null-brothers" in Magdeburg. At that time, according to the letter, Luther had made Storm's acquaintance at the home of Dr. Paul Mosshauer, where Storm had been a guest "now and then." (See *W. A., Br.,* II, 563.)

It is generally accepted that the Nullbrothers were the Brethren of the Common Life and that this experience in Martin's life was during 1497-98. What has not been so clear is whether Luther attended a school operated by the Magdeburg Brethren themselves or whether he attended a school where some of them simply were teachers. If the latter be the case, the school is thought to have been the cathedral school; for the city school was not founded until the 1520's, and it is generally felt unlikely that he attended one of the church schools in Magdeburg.

Thus, there have been two main opinions as to what school Luther attended in Magdeburg: (1) the Brethren's own school, or (2) the cathedral school. Since the time when these views were argued respectively by E. Barnikol (1917) and O. Scheel (1921), scholars in the field have usually identified themselves with one or the other of these positions. Recently, however, there has been a tendency in certain renowned publications to disallow the first option. The present brief study proposes to glance at several of these publications and also at some important works taking an opposite position. No attempt is made to be comprehensive, and only publications appearing within the past two decades or so will be treated.

In America, the viewpoint of Ernest G. Schwiebert, *Luther and His Times* (St. Louis, Mo., 1950) must immediately be taken into account, even though Schwiebert makes only brief mention of Luther's stay in Magdeburg (pages 117-122). The reason for Schwiebert's importance in this connection is the high esteem in which his book is held and the wide dissemination it has consequently received. Indeed, *Luther and His Times* is a work of highest scholarly merit, well deserving the reputation it has received. The relevant statement (on page 119) is as follows:

> The Brethren of the Common Life did not have a school of their own [in Magdeburg], but three or four of their number were teaching in the *Domschule*, the Cathedral School, for centuries famous all over northwest Germany. Could it have been here that the young Luther went to school in Magdeburg and could rightly say he had gone to school to the *Nullbrueder?*

Likewise, the viewpoint of Harold J. Grimm, *The Reformation Era* (New York, 1954), must be taken into account, inasmuch as this excellent book has been widely used as a textbook for courses in the Reformation. On page 91 of this publication Grimm expresses essentially the same view as that given by Schwiebert.

R. R. Post has for years been recognized as an outstanding Dutch authority on the Brethren of the Common Life and their educational work. His recent book in English—*The Modern Devotion* (Leiden, 1968)—will undoubtedly enjoy a popularity in America beyond that of his various Dutch publications. This is a comprehensive work of some 700 pages, and offers valuable correctives for those who tend to overemphasize the contributions made by the Brethren of the Common Life. On the other hand, it is somewhat marred by its polemical nature. Post feels, for example, that various scholars—such as P. Mestwerdt, Lewis W. Spitz, G. Bonet-Maury, A. Renaudet, and A. Hyma (see pages 1-17)—have overestimated the educational work and influence of the Brethren of the Common Life. Even though Post himself calls attention to certain schools operated by the Brethren, he takes pains to point out that these were late in the history of the Brotherhood and usually not so significant as is sometimes thought. With but one or two exceptions, according to him, the Brethren began to establish schools of their own only after about 1480. They had, of course, had dormitories for students prior to this.

As for Magdeburg (dealt with on pages 628-630), Post feels that the Brethren of the Common Life could not in 1497 have had a school there sufficiently advanced "for a boy of thirteen," nor could Brothers have been teachers in the cathedral school (page 629). The city would not have tolerated a school of the Brothers since they were "newcomers and none too popular." Also, the Magdeburg house was still in the hands of the Hildesheim Brothers, who "never had their own school in Hildesheim" (*ibidem*). Since "it is difficult to imagine that the *fraters* from Hildesheim were competent to teach successfully," the "only remaining solution is that the young Martin boarded with the Brothers and went to school elsewhere" (page 630).

The polemical setting of Post's book is unfortunate, as I have mentioned. It leads the author to overlook or underemphasize certain important data because of his overemphasis on other, equally important facts. Also, it is unfortunate that Post has failed to take into account recent treatments of the educational work of the Brethren of the Common Life by W. Landeen (1953), J. Henkel (1962), and A. Hyma (1965), which will be noticed below.

More sweeping than the statements of either Schwiebert or Post are remarks by H. Baeyens, *Begrip en Probleem van de Renaissance: Bijdrage tot de geschiedenis van hun onststaan en tot hun kunsthistorische Omschrijving* (Leuven, 1952), page 263. He feels that in the world of education the Brethren played the role of assistants. "Real teachers they were not," he says, "and the schools in which they cooperated were usually city schools." If Baeyens is correct, obviously there was no school of the Brethren of the Common Life in Magdeburg, for the Brotherhood simply had no schools at all!

Baeyens' statement may be dismissed at once. Various scholars, including R. R. Post, have proved that in a number of places the Brethren of the Common Life did have schools. Very important in this connection is the careful work by Julia S. Henkel, *An Historical Study of the Educational Contributions of the Brethren of the Common Life* (Ph.D. Dissertation; University of Pittsburgh, 1962). A brief sampling of the kind of material brought to light by Mrs. Henkel is also presented in her chapter "School Organizational Patterns of the Brethren of the Common Life," pages 323-338 in the Albert Hyma Festschrift volume *Dawn of Modern Civilization* (Ann Arbor, Mich., 1962; 2nd ed., 1964), edited by the present writer. This chapter has now been reprinted in *Essays on the Northern Renaissance* (Ann Arbor, Mich., 1968), pages 35-50. Mrs. Henkel reveals the educational achievements of the Brethren to have been considerably greater than what Post assumes. She also shatters Baeyens' assumption.

There is no question but that the Brethren of the Common Life did indeed have schools! But did they have one in Magdeburg when Luther arrived there in 1497?

In contrast to the views of Schwiebert and Post, as noted above, is that of William M. Landeen. This scholar has presented a penetrating analysis of Luther's stay in Magdeburg in his "The *Devotio Moderna* in Germany," Part III, in *Research Studies of the State College of Washington*, Volume XXI (1953), pages 302-309. Landeen quotes the relevant part of Luther's letter to Claus Storm and couples with it a letter written in 1503 by Nicholas Dorsten, rector of the Brethren's Magdeburg house, to the procurator of the Brethren in Hildesheim. Dorsten's letter refers to certain boys recommended from Hildesheim as being accepted "by us." It also requests prayer for "John Dorsten so that he may be given wisdom to labor well on behalf of the boys, according to the grace given him." Landeen argues that it is unlikely that parents in Hildesheim would send sons to the Magdeburg Brethren simply for religious instruction, inasmuch as the Hildesheim Brethren were themselves engaged in that very work. Rather, the letter points to "a more definite program of teaching" and even names "the particular brother who supervised the boys in this work" (page 306). Landeen also suggests that although this letter does not definitely speak about a school

in Magdeburg, Luther's letter to Storm does tell us about such
a school:

> Luther does tell us about such a school. As noted, he
> said specifically that he "went to school to the Null-
> brothers" in Magdeburg, together with Hans Reinecke. It
> is difficult to conceive of this language as meaning anything
> other than that he attended a school operated by the
> Nullbrothers. The fact that the Nullbrothers operated the
> school he remembered and stressed. If this was the
> cathedral school, as has been asserted, then the brethren
> must have been in full control of that institution, for
> Luther singles out the Nullbrothers as conducting the
> school which he attended. Whatever the school, the
> Nullbrothers dominated it, and that fact Luther remem-
> bered. His language is clear and unequivocal. (*Ibidem*)

Landeen further points out (page 307) that in Magdeburg
Luther probably resided, not with the Brethren, but at the home
of Dr. Paul Mosshauer. Luther's letter to Claus Storm would
imply as much. At that home, it will be recalled, he had met
Storm, who had been a guest there "now and then." Also,
Landeen believes that Ratzeberger's account of Luther's experience of an illness one Friday fits better into the life of a private
home than into that of a dormitory. Luther had suffered a
severe fever, which was broken only when he crawled on hands
and knees to the kitchen for cold water while the rest of the
folk were away at church.

Julia S. Henkel, on pages 207, 208, of her afore-mentioned
dissertation, likewise takes the position that Luther attended a
school actually operated by the Brethren of the Common Life
in Magdeburg. In her opinion, the wording of Luther's letter
to Claus Storm would not make sense otherwise. Why, she
wonders, should Luther be considered vague here, whereas
he usually was not vague in saying what he meant? Although
Landeen's is the more basic discussion of the problem, Henkel's
attention to it merits notice because of her placing it within
the setting of a comprehensive study dealing specifically with
the educational contributions of the Brethren of the Common
Life.

Although R. R. Post has accused Albert Hyma of over-emphasizing the contributions of the Brethren of the Common Life (see *The Modern Devotion,* pages 15-17) as these were presented in Hyma's original edition of *The Christian Renaissance: A History of the "Devotio Moderna"* (Grand Rapids, Mich., 1924), Hyma himself is now more emphatic on those contributions than he was in 1924. In a new edition of this book (published in Hamden, Conn., in 1965), Hyma notes that in the original edition of *The Christian Renaissance* he did "not do proper justice to the educational contributions by the Brethren of the Common Life" (page 609). He mentions the work of Mrs. Henkel and calls attention to the fact that both in Deventer and Amersfoort the Brethren did more than he had previously assumed. He also indicates that even "more interesting has been the study of the school operated by the Brethren in Magdeburg, which was located in their own house. Here Martin Luther spent one year" (page 610).

Hyma's conclusions, it must be added, are not entirely based on work done by such scholars as Landeen (who was a doctoral student of Hyma's) and Mrs. Henkel (who during the preparation of her dissertation consulted him on a number of important points), as might be assumed by a casual reading of the relevant portion of the new edition of *The Christian Renaissance.* In 1957, the present writer consulted a long manuscript prepared by Professor Hyma on the Brethren's educational contributions. This excellent manuscript was the product of Hyma's own first-hand investigation of the subject. Unfortunately, it has not been published.

The foregoing sampling of recent research would indicate that the door should not be closed on the possibility that Luther attended a school operated by the Brethren of the Common Life in Magdeburg. That possibility should still be retained as a live option.

In closing this study, one further point deserves brief attention: As Luther went to school "to the Nullbrothers" in Magdeburg, how much of an impact did these Brethren of the Common Life have on him? Opinion on this question divides along lines somewhat different from those noted above. Certain recent European writers tend to minimize the impact. So, for example, does Franz Lau. On page 37 of the English edition of his book entitled *Luther* (Philadelphia, 1963), translated from the German edition of 1959 by Robert H. Fischer, Lau pays tribute to the educational work of the Brethren of the Common Life but nevertheless warns against over-estimating the influence of the Magdeburg Brethren on Luther. A more cursory reference is given in Heinrich Böhmer's English edition of his Luther biography entitled *Martin Luther: Road to Reformation*, which appeared as a Meridian "Living Age Books" paperback in 1957 and was translated from Böhmer's *Der Junge Luther* by John W. Doberstein and Theodore G. Tappert. On page 17 of this English edition we read that "Martin went to the school of the '*Nullbrüder*,' the Brethren of the Common Life," but also that it "does not appear that he was strongly influenced in any way by the Brethren." On page 630 of his *The Modern Devotion*, R. R. Post states that Luther's stay in Magdeburg "was only short" and that "although Luther as a child was able to see something of the Devotion of the Brothers one can scarcely attribute any permanent influence to this brief contact."

On the other side are certain American writers, including the present one (see, for example, page 67, above, in my chapter on "Luther's Condemnation of the Rostock New Testament"). Some of these writers attribute much significance to the contact which Luther had with the Magdeburg Brethren of the Common Life, whether that contact was with them in their own school or in some other school. Schwiebert, for example, has suggested that "in all likelihood it was at Magdeburg that Luther made his discovery of the Bible" (*op. cit.*, page 119). This viewpoint is shared by Albert Hyma, *Martin Luther and the Luther Film of 1953* (Ann Arbor, Mich., 1957), page 12, and *New Light on Martin Luther* (Grand Rapids, Mich., 1958), page 12. Hyma goes on to say (page 13 in both editions) that in Magdeburg "Luther must have obtained what his parents had hoped he would find, namely devotion in the religious sense."